W9-ATU-056

Collaboration

Collaboration

Uniting Our Gifts in Ministry

Loughlan Sofield, ST

Carroll Juliano, SHCJ

ave maria press   Notre Dame, IN

© 2000 by Ave Maria Press, Inc.

All rights reserved. No part of this book may be used or reproduced in any manner whatsoever, except in the case of reprints in the context of reviews, without written permission from Ave Maria Press, Inc., P.O. Box 428, Notre Dame, IN 46556.

Founded in 1865, Ave Maria Press is a ministry of the Indiana Province of Holy Cross.

www.avemariapress.com

ISBN-10 0-87793-683-8   ISBN-13 978-0-87793-683-1
Cover and text design by Brian C. Conley
Printed and bound in the United States of America.

Library of Congress Cataloging-in-Publication Data

Sofield, Loughlan.
    Collaboration : uniting our gifts in ministry / Loughlan Sofield and Carroll Juliano.
        p. cm.
    Includes bibliographical references.
    ISBN 0-87793-683-8 (pbk.)
    1. Cooperative ministry. 2. Priesthood, Universal. 3. Lay ministry--Catholic Church. 4. Catholic Church--Clergy. 5. Pastoral theology--Catholic Church.   I. Juliano, Carroll. II. Title.

BX2347 .S64   2000
253--dc21

00-008889
CIP

To our parents
Mary and George Sofield
Eleanor and Jerry Juliano

we dedicate this book with continued love and gratitude

Acknowledgments

Throughout our thirteen-year relationship, the staff of Ave Maria has been unbelievably supportive and encouraging to us. It was at the invitation of Frank Cunningham and Bob Hamma that this project came into existence. We thank them for their continued friendship and assistance.

A project of this magnitude is not possible without the assistance of many people. We wish to thank the following who assisted in myriad ways, from researching difficult-to-find quotes to offering critical suggestions: Louise Bond, SNJM; Frank Ferrante, CMF; Sheila Garcia; Patrick Hart, OCSO; Amy Hoey, RSM; Brian Jarboe; Melinda Keane, SHCJ; H. Richard McCord; Hilary Mettes, ST; Ann Rehrauer, OSF; Raymond Sofield; and Gerald Woodman.

Chapter 11, "Collaborative Ministry in Practice," would not exist without the willingness of William Bausch, Mary Bourdon, RJM, and Marge Hebert, MSC, who graciously agreed to be interviewed.

We are especially indebted to Bishop Howard Hubbard for contributing the foreword. His willingness to accept this request in the midst of his demanding schedule is a further indication of his personal commitment to collaborative ministry.

Contents

Foreword 9

Introduction 11

1. *A Model for Collaborative Ministry* 17

2. *Myths of Collaborative Ministry* 31

3. *Evolution of Collaborative Ministry* 39

4. *Obstacles to Collaborative Ministry* 51

5. *Readiness for Collaborative Ministry* 73

6. *Spirituality for Collaborative Ministry* 85

7. *Group Leadership* 103

8. *Conflict* 123

9. *Confrontation* 139

10. *Structure and Process for Collaborative Ministry* . . .147

11. *Collaborative Ministry in Practice* 163

Epilogue: *Collaborative Leadership: A Challenge to All* . . .177

Bibliography 183

Sources 186

Foreword

We have stepped into this new millennium as a people and a church still becoming. We carry with us the stories, experiences, and relationships which have molded and shaped us as disciples of Jesus. We have grown more comfortable with our pilgrim status and a servant model of leadership. We come with hope and expectation seasoned by both success and failure. We are learning to pack the essentials of ministry—faith, compassion, forgiveness, prayer, collaboration, and mission—and we are leaving behind what clouds the vision and detours the journey.

As those called to ministry we have gained confidence and direction from a renewed theology of baptism. We have discovered and affirmed the gifts given to us for the sake of the mission. And we are learning that only when we are open to collaboration and interdependence will we really build the reign of God in this space and time.

As the world grows more complex, time more rapid, and needs more numerous, we have discovererd that we can only meet the challenges we face when all the gifts given by our creator God are unleashed to work in harmony for the common good. Those called to leadership become like the master weaver blending multiple threads into a magnificent tapestry, or the conductor inviting all the sounds into a beautiful symphony.

There are none in church leadership today who have given more commitment, passion, and scholarship to a visioin of collaborative ministry than Br. Loughlan Sofield and Sr. Carroll Juliano. They have been and continue to be guides for all in the church today, and for me personally. They call us to be a church which is more alive, apostolic, and faith-filled by committing ourselves to "release all the gifts in ministry for the sake of the mission of Jesus Christ."

The lived experience of the past decade has taught us that collaboration is complex and difficult. It requires "commitment, patience, humor, and hard work." What is born of the effort is a "community of love, life and truth that witnesses to God's presence among us." This book takes us beyond the question of whether we will collaborate or not to skills-based strategies on how we as individuals and communities can move collaboration from an ideal to a reality. It likewise offers us an assessment tool for personal reflection on our own readiness and capacity for collaborative ministry, calling us to a deeper spirituality and an openness to conversion.

The research of the authors demonstrates that collaborative ministry is essential to diverse organizations within the church. The chapters on group leadership, dealing with conflict, and confrontation provide essential skills and strategies for all in ministry today. The authors raise the concern that our formation programs and processes have not given adequate emphasis to an understanding of the growth and development of group process which is essential to ministry and mission.

We who are leaders in our contemporary church—laypersons, members of religious communities, deacons, priests, and bishops—have been given a gift, a challenge, and a blueprint in *Collaboration: Uniting Our Gifts in Ministry*. It is my prayer and hope that I will continue to be formed and shaped by the prophetic vision of this book and that the church will continue to be renewed through the giftedness of each and every person called by baptism to build the reign of God.

Howard J. Hubbard
Bishop of Albany
Easter 2000

Introduction

Every generation in the church faces unique challenges. The challenge for today's church is to give birth to the vision of collaborative ministry proclaimed by the Second Vatican Council.

Over the last twenty years it has been our privilege to work with tens of thousands of Christians who are actively struggling to give birth to that vision. Out of these experiences have come the following convictions:

1. The church founded by Jesus Christ is a church of and on a mission. It is an apostolic church; an evangelizing church.
2. The greater the collaboration, the greater the growth of this apostolic church.
3. Failure to develop a more collaborative approach to ministry condemns the church to mere survival. A non-collaborative church is a church of maintenance rather than a church of mission.
4. Collaborative ministry is messy, sometimes difficult, and at times, painful.

Most people are quick to affirm, at least intellectually, the first three convictions. However, failure to acknowledge and embrace the final conviction, the messiness, thwarts collaborative models and retards the growth of mission.

It has been our good fortune to work with dioceses, parishes, educational institutions, and other Christian groups seeking to become more collaborative. At times we have been edified and inspired by their efforts. At other times we have been discouraged and dejected. The edification and inspiration resulted from encountering deeply committed Christians who combined their conviction of the need for collaborative ministry with a strong commitment to develop the necessary attitude and skills. Discouragement and dejection arose where we encountered individuals and groups unwilling to make the long-term commitment to work through the messiness of collaboration in order to carry out the mission of Jesus Christ more effectively.

One hindrance to a long-term commitment is the belief that collaborative ministry is little more than an ephemeral dream, a passing fad. Those who hold such beliefs view collaborative ministry as an ideal concept incapable of being achieved, one that is out of reach. This negative attitude does not reflect our experience. We have been blessed both to hear and see many examples of successful collaboration in numerous countries and continents. Collaborative ministry is working!

There are parishes with whom we have journeyed for years. They have committed themselves to the slow but rewarding task of growth in collaborative ministry. Sometimes their journey has been strewn with emotional land mines. At other times there have been the unexpected hope-filled examples of grace in action. The parishioners have reaped the fruits of that commitment. Long-term commitment has resulted in parishes that are more alive, more apostolic and more faith-filled. These are the parishes which most fully reflect the mission, as described by the United States Conference of Catholic Bishops (hereafter called the USCCB, until 2000 known as the National Conference of Catholic Bishops or NCCB).

> The mission of the church is not directed solely at itself, but at nurturing and forming people who are called by God, so that, led by the Spirit they might contribute to the sanctification of the world (SDL, p. 22).

This vision is not restricted to parishes only. We have likewise encountered dioceses where the diocesan bishops, after carefully listening to and reflecting on the needs of the people, committed themselves and their diocesan resources to a long-term process of the development of collaborative ministry. In some instances diocesan bishops have even made collaborative ministry the priority of the diocese.

In the United States, Canada, and Australia we have been privileged to work with educational institutions at the local, regional, diocesan, and national levels. After an initial introduction to collaborative ministry, many of these institutions committed themselves to concrete steps in order to insure their continued growth as a collaborative organization.

While we have mentioned parish, diocese, and educational institutions, the successful examples of collaborative ministry are not restricted to these three arenas. There are also countless Christian organizations and centers which have made collaborative ministry a major goal of their organization.

In myriad examples, collaborative ministry has furthered the mission of Jesus Christ. Collaborative ministry is not just a good idea because "many hands make light work" but because it is of the very nature of the church. Or, as Roger Cardinal Mahony of Los Angeles has said,

> Collaboration is necessary not only to achieve our goals more effectively, but more important to live out our witness as church more authentically (ROL, p. 8).

In that same document, Mahony identified a number of reasons why collaborative ministry is essential:

> Our common baptismal vocation, our mutual need of each other's charisms and our co-responsibility for the church's ministry, impel us to a life of collaboration (ROL, p. 8).

At this time, the question is not *whether* we will develop collaborative structures, but rather *how*. The time is long past to debate the value and merits of working together for the kingdom.

Collaborative ministry is generally espoused by many people in church ministry today. Many even perceive themselves as models of collaboration. Recent documents issued by various church bodies have spoken of the value and necessity of collaboration. However, at times, there appears to be much more rhetoric about collaboration than actual collaborative activity. Frequently, the practice lags dramatically behind the theory. Occasionally, the primary focus of collaboration is decision-making, rather than ministry.

Our publisher, Ave Maria Press, has requested that we share how we have seen collaborative ministry evolve since our first work, *Collaborative Ministry: Skills and Guidelines*. Our goal in writing this book is to describe where we have seen collaborative ministry working and what we believe is required to further the collaborative ideal. Included in this book are numerous quotes and excerpts from those entrusted with the teaching ministry of the church. The reference to numerous documents shows the strength of conviction on the part of church leaders throughout the world. There is a literal explosion of church documents which advocate collaboration. Sadly, there does not appear to be a similar explosion of practical texts that transfer this theory into practice. Often, too, the implementation lags far behind the articulation.

The church documents quoted in this book are referenced in the section identified as "Sources." Included in the sources are documents from the Vatican as well as from national and state conferences of bishops. In addition, we have listed talks given by Pope John Paul II and pastorals published by individual bishops. Any books or articles referred to in the text are included in the bibliography rather than footnoted.

Most of the resources are from the Catholic tradition. The resources are vast, so we have restricted ourselves to a representative sampling. However, it is not only the Catholic church that is advocating collaborative ministry. A recent publication of the World Council of Churches exclaims,

> All are called to be Christ's agents of transformation in the world, serving in different ways and means according to one's gifts and inclinations (LCW).

This book attempts to combine what has remained constant during the last decade with regard to collaborative ministry, and to develop those areas in which experience has provided us with greater clarity and further insight.

While this book contains material included in our previous work on collaborative ministry, it also provides new developments and content. Two frequently asked questions provide the focus: "What is collaborative ministry?" and "How do we make it work?"

Chapter 1 presents a model we have developed to foster collaborative ministry, "the Four C's." In Chapter 2 we introduce some myths regarding collaborative ministry that can impede its development. Chapter 3 introduces the reader to some ecclesial documents which are helping to concrete a sometimes nebulous understanding of collaborative ministry. Chapter 4 identifies some of the key obstacles to collaborative ministry. Developmental readiness for collaborative ministry is developed in Chapter 5 and a spirituality for collaborative ministry is presented in Chapter 6. Chapters 7, 8, and 9 focus on three of the major skills required for collaborative ministry: group leadership, dealing with conflict, and learning effective ways to confront. The process and structures which facilitate collaborative ministry are contained in Chapter 10. The final chapter gleans the learnings from three collaborative projects and presents some research conducted in the not-for-profit sector. The Epilogue includes challenges for collaboration for all the people of God.

Throughout the book we have included reflection questions. These questions can be used individually or in a group. Conscientious attention to these questions will help to move the reader to the personal conversion needed for collaborative ministry.

This book is not the last word on collaborative ministry but simply the next word. Hopefully, it will serve as a catalyst to invite others to share their experiences and insights as to what makes collaborative ministry successful.

Collaboration is difficult. It requires commitment, patience, humility, and hard work. Nonetheless, it forms us into the community of love, life, and truth that witnesses to God's presence among us.

1

A Model for Collaborative Ministry

What is collaborative ministry? How do you implement collaborative ministry? At a recent national meeting, there were more workshops on collaboration, collaborative ministry, and collaborative leadership than any other topic. Discussion among the presenters revealed that there was not a universal meaning for the term. Clarification of the term *collaborative ministry* is fundamental. When a common understanding of meaning is absent, ambiguity reigns. Ambiguity generally produces anxiety, tension, and conflict. Anxiety, tension, and conflict, in turn, often impede collaborative ministry.

Since a common understanding of the term is the starting point, we begin with a working definition of collaborative ministry. This will be followed by a description of the levels of collaboration. Finally, a model for collaboration, the Four C's, will be introduced.

Collaboration Defined

Collaboration is defined as "the identification, release, and union of all the *gifts* in *ministry* for the sake of *mission*." This definition has three key elements. First, the essence of collaborative ministry is gift. Second, collaboration is never an end in itself: it is a vehicle for ministry. Third, the goal of collaborative ministry is always the mission of Jesus Christ.

Gift—Ministry—Mission

This chapter will first identify four levels in the evolution of collaborative ministry. Second, we will offer a concrete model, "The Four C's," for effective implementation of collaborative ministry.

Collaboration grows and evolves through a rather clear, predictable, and developmental process. We have identified four levels of collaboration: co-existence, communication, cooperation, and true collaboration. After you review the four levels, determine your group's level. Once done, the group can decide whether there is a desire to grow beyond this level.

Table 1.1	*Levels of Collaboration*
	Level one—Co-existence
	Level two—Communication
	Level three—Cooperation
	Level four—Collaboration

The first level of collaboration is *co-existence*. At this level the individuals or groups identify with one another in some general way. They share some common history, mission, or membership. However, the individuals or groups exist separately and independently of each other. They may be on the same staff or faculty, but for all intents and purposes that relationship exacts no mutual expectations or accountability. The only point of connection is their common designation as staff, team, or faculty. An example is a chancery staff where each office and department conducts its own ministry without any reference to what is transpiring in the other departments.

The second level, *communication*, occurs when there is an explicit decision to enter into some mutual interaction and dialogue. At this level the individuals/programs/institutions have mutual access to each other. This increased communication involves more interaction among the members and sharing of information, such as calendars, programs, and activities. Attendance at meetings or workshops can lead to discussing matters of common and mutual interest. Often, this initial sharing of information leads to a deeper level, the sharing of ideals and values. From this comes a growing realization of bondedness. For instance, when the chancery staff begins having joint meetings to share information, this level of communication can develop.

Increased communication leads to an understanding that while each person or unit is different and distinct, each has the same purpose and mission. This realization results in the separate entities working together and cooperating with one another.

This *cooperation* is the distinguishing characteristic of the third level. Through cooperation comes a growing awareness that individuals and programs do not exist in isolation, but have an impact on each other, either positively or negatively. This dynamic is a movement toward interdependence. This can again be seen by returning to the example of the chancery staff. One department describes their efforts in light of the mission of the diocese and the other departments decide how they can support this effort. At this level there is usually one group which is the "lead agent" for a project and the others are seen as auxiliary to the major group.

When interdependence becomes a reality there is a readiness, and often an ardent desire, to move toward the fourth level, true *collaboration*. This level is characterized by a number of realities. First, the group acknowledges, articulates, and experiences ownership of a common mission. Second, there is a desire to work together for a common goal. "Turf" issues are relegated to a lower status. The desire to collaborate, rather than compete, arises as the driving force. Turf and competition are replaced by a spirit of mutuality and partnership. Third, there is a decision to identify, value, and unite the various gifts that each possesses. Individuals and groups acknowledge the gifts they bring to the common mission and are able to affirm the gifts that others bring. Collaboration occurs when all the different gifts are freely joined together in ministry for the common purpose of furthering the mission of Jesus Christ.

Table 1.2	*Characteristics of Achieving Level Four of Collaboration*
	• Acknowledges, articulates, and experiences a sense of ownership of a common mission.
	• Achieves a sense of unity accompanied by a desire to work together for a common goal.
	• Decides to identify, value, and bring together the various gifts.

Using the description of the four levels from co-existence to collaboration, reflect on the following questions:

1. At which level do I perceive myself and the group to which I belong? Do I/we have a desire to grow to another level? If so, how can the group grow to the next level?
2. How would those we serve assess our ministry in terms of these levels? How can we foster continued growth?
3. To what degree do we witness a collaborative relationship? How can we adequately and honestly determine that? Are we open to being challenged to further development?

The Practical Steps to Collaborative Ministry

The primary way to become truly collaborative is to focus on "the Four C's" of collaboration: clarification, conviction, commitment, and capacity/capability. After reading, reflect on the implications of these elements for yourself and for the group with whom you collaborate.

Table 1.3	*The Four C's of Collaboration* Clarification Conviction Commitment Capacity/Capability

Clarification

Collaboration is a word that has come to have as many meanings as there are people discussing it. An obstacle to collaborative ministry is the absence of a common understanding. Any group who wishes to become more collaborative must first spend time discussing what the term means to each of the individuals within the group or unit. After the initial sharing, there is need for the group to determine a corporate understanding of collaboration. Failure to arrive at a common understanding of collaboration will result in frustration and inevitable conflict.

The United States Conference of Catholic Bishops has commented on the frustration experienced when people do not share a common understanding of collaborative ministry:

> Women and men alike told us that collaboration is a major issue for them. They noted the successes they had achieved as well as the difficulties, especially when people do not share the same understanding of collaboration (FWD, p. 17).

Collaboration is a form of ministry that is based completely on the concept of *gift*. The goal of collaborative ministry is to further the mission of Jesus Christ. The criteria to measure the effectiveness of any collaborative effort is the extent that it furthers the reign of God. The essence of collaborative ministry is the identification, release, and union of all the gifts in the Christian community. This statement emphasizes the fact that 100 percent of the people of God are both gifted and called. Pope John Paul II stresses this concept of a universal call:

> It is essential for us to understand that Jesus has a specific task in life for each and every one of us. Each one of us is handpicked, called by name, called by Jesus. There is no one among us who does not have a divine vocation (HG).

Any collaborative project must develop a process for clearly identifying the gifts of the individuals or groups involved. Next, a frank and candid exploration must be undertaken to determine what, in the individuals or in the system, is preventing the gifts from being placed at the service of the gospel. Finally, there is need to determine how the gifts can be joined together to accomplish the mission.

The concept of gift is at the heart of collaboration. Collaboration based on any criteria other than giftedness is artificial.

Table 1.4

The Essence of Collaborative Ministry
Gifts—Ministry—Mission
- Identification
- Release
- Union

John Bathersby, the archbishop of Brisbane, Australia, has issued several excellent documents—including *Becoming More Collaborative*—in which he describes, rather than defines, collaboration. Bathersby names the elements of collaboration as:

- working together in partnership;
- shared responsibility, mutuality, and interdependence;
- a church of baptismal equality;
- empowerment—empowering people to recognize and use their gifts;
- People of God—in community;
- shared and servant leadership.

Bathersby reinforces the threefold aspect of collaboration: gift, ministry, and mission by declaring that collaboration is the utilization of "our gifts in partnership with one another to carry out the mission of Jesus in the world" (BMC). Like many other church leaders, Bathersby emphasizes collaboration's place "in the world."

Those who accept this description will have three barometers—expressed by the following questions—by which they can evaluate their collaborative efforts:

1. Do we assign the roles and functions based on a discernment of gifts?
2. Is our effort truly ministry, i.e., focused on serving others rather than simply deepening our communal relationships?
3. In what ways does our collaborative effort further the mission of Jesus Christ?

Bishop Howard Hubbard of Albany, New York describes the church as, "a community of collaborative ministry" (GPP). He recommends three tasks to bring this community of collaborative ministry into existence. They are to:

1. help every baptized person realize that as a result of baptism each one is called to holiness and ministry;
2. assist every person to discover their gifts and talents, and help in discerning where and how they can use those gifts in service and in ministry;
3. challenge all leaders to see their primary role as empowering and animating the gifts of the entire community.

In the variety of definitions and descriptions of collaborative ministry noted above, there is an emphasis on the concept of *all*. The challenge of collaborative ministry is to mobilize the gifts that God has placed within the Christian community. The goal of true collaboration is not limited to a small group working together in ministry. It is the animation of the entire body in ministry for the sake of mission.

In summary, collaboration is a way of performing *ministry*. It is completely based on the identification, release, and union of all the *gifts* in the Christian community for the purpose of continuing the *mission* of Jesus Christ.

We have shared our understanding of collaborative ministry. Any group who wishes to become more collaborative is encouraged to spend time clarifying their common understanding of what constitutes collaborative ministry.

Conviction

Once a group successfully clarifies its common understanding, the next step is to discover whether its members are convinced of the value in ministering collaboratively. Collaborative ministry is messy: it forces us to deal with such "demons" as anger, conflict, confrontation, and hostility, as well as threatening issues of termination, sexuality, and faith sharing. Commitment to the process of collaborative ministry will endure to the degree that those involved have a strong internal conviction of its importance and value. Without this conviction, a group will abandon its collaborative efforts as soon as the messiness begins leaking into daily encounters.

A direct way to ascertain the level of conviction is to ask the members to identify reasons why they are convinced of the value of collaboration. The inability to generate sufficient reasons for conviction will result in no collaboration.

In general, the reasons for conviction fall into two broad categories: theological and practical. The theological convictions for collaborative ministry are rooted in a theology of the Trinity, the nature of sacrament, and the gospel call to *communio*. (Communio is a relatively recent term that expands the concept of community to a deeper and more profound reality.)

Sometimes it is often the practical reasons that finally move people to action. Some have claimed that "necessity is the mother of theology." The practical reasons for collaboration are numerous: e.g., it's fun, more can be accomplished, no one person has all the gifts, the synergy produced by the utilization of a variety of gifts is energizing, and other equally positive, valid reasons. Once clarity and conviction are established the next question is: how committed are the members of the group to collaborative ministry?

Commitment

No person is unconditionally committed to collaborative ministry. Rather, everyone is ambivalent. Even those who are staunchly convinced of the value of collaborative ministry experience some stirrings of resistance. Resistance is related to the fears and obstacles that confront anyone attempting to collaborate. The primary challenges are to identify, discuss, and attempt to resolve those fears and obstacles.

Many people are more comfortable focusing on the obstacles which are external to them. It is less personally threatening to blame a lack of commitment to collaboration on the hierarchical church, the sponsoring institutions, or the inadequacies of co-workers. However, commitment to collaboration is possible only when one is willing to confront the fears and obstacles which are internal and personal.

We have identified (see Table 1.5) the fears and obstacles which emerge most frequently.

Table 1.5 *Major Obstacles to Collaboration*
1. low self-esteem
2. arrogance
3. burnout
4. hostility
5. inability or unwillingness to deal with conflict
6. unwillingness to deal with loss, termination, and separation
7. a lack of integrated sexuality

Table 1.5 *(continued)*	8. a lack of knowledge of one's own gifts or the gifts of one's co-workers 9. an unwillingness or fear of sharing faith

The most central and profound obstacle to greater collaboration is low self-esteem (see, for example, *Design for Wholeness*, pp. 81-109). When the self-esteem of an individual or group is low, hostility and competition ensue. Both hostility and excessive competition militate against collaboration. Conversely, when individuals and groups possess a high level of self-esteem, there is greater commitment to collaboration and the collaborative efforts are more effective.

Identification of fears and obstacles is the first step. Here collaborative efforts can falter because commitment demands change and even radical conversion. Given the fact that most organisms—including individuals, groups, and even the church—protect themselves from change, this step in the process is a challenging one.

What are the major fears and obstacles which prevent you and the members of your group from greater collaboration? Have you identified, discussed, and attempted to resolve these obstacles? Chapter 4 offers a fuller development of these obstacles.

Capacity/Capability

There are some instances where time has been spent defining the meaning of collaboration and concurrently cogent and profound reasons for collaboration have been identified. Even the difficult process of identifying and resolving obstacles has been undertaken. But little progress in the journey toward collaboration has occurred. Collaboration demands more than an act of volition. It demands that those involved possess the capacity and the capability to collaborate.

There are four major areas to address in developing capacity and capability: skills, spirituality, process, and developmental readiness.

	Elements of Capacity and Capability
Table 1.6	• Skills • Spirituality • Process • Developmental Readiness

Skills

Among the skills required for collaboration are: group leadership, conflict resolution and management, confrontation, and discernment of gifts. Competency in these skills is needed, not only by those in designated leadership positions, but also by anyone involved in collaborative ministry. According to the work by the Committee on Women in Society and in the Church:

> Collaboration requires certain skills which can be learned. These skills include communication, the ability to work with groups, and the ability to deal with diversity in its various forms. Conflict resolution and management skills are also essential. People often see conflict as "unchristian" and seek to avoid it. The wise community will ensure that some of its members have the training and skills to help the group deal positively with conflict so that it becomes a means for learning and growth (FWD, p. 20).

The lack of competency in these skills results in feelings of incompetency and frustration. Skill development is not acquired in a single workshop but takes training, practice, and often supervision. Chapters 7, 8, and 9 expand on these skills.

Spirituality

Spirituality is our relationship with God as it affects every aspect of our lives. Spirituality, then, should lead a person into loving service. Pope John Paul II commented on the relationship between spirituality and service. Two citations follow:

> Christianity is not only a religion of knowledge, of contemplation, it is a religion of God's action and of man (or woman's) action (CTH, p. 128).

> . . . Faith is a lived knowledge of Christ. . . . A word in
> any event is not truly received until it passes into action,
> until it is put into practice. Faith is a decision involving
> one's whole existence (SV, #88).

No action is truly ministry unless it flows from spirituality, one's relationship with God. While there is no definitive description of what constitutes a collaborative spirituality, essential elements can be delineated. First, it must be shared, that is, a person must be willing to engage in faith sharing, allowing others to know one's experiences and encounters with God. A spirituality for collaboration must be appropriate for the unique individual in all aspects of his or her life; basically, spirituality must "fit" who you are. Finally, spirituality must move a person to action. A collaborative spirituality leads a person toward compassionate action and acts of forgiveness that witness to the presence of Jesus Christ. Chapter 6 expands on some aspects of an active spirituality for collaborative ministry.

Process

The existence of a definite process will enable a group to move through the levels from coexistence to true collaboration. The process contains a number of elements: a common, gospel-oriented, collaborative vision, a method for identifying gifts, a structure which assures that the gifts are used for ministry, a clarification of roles and authority, and a system for accountability and evaluation. While each of these elements is essential, the most important element is the identification or discernment of gifts.

There are numerous processes of gift discernment. The particular model we have used successfully in a variety of settings is described in our previous book, *Building Community*. Chapter 10 of this work develops the concept of gift discernment more fully.

Developmental Readiness

Called and Gifted for the Third Millennium, a document on laity published by the USCCB, challenges every member of the church to be more collaborative. The bishops remind each person of her or his four calls as a Christian: to holiness, to community, to mission and ministry, and to Christian maturity.

The issue of maturity can easily be overlooked when contemplating collaboration. Yet, the question must be asked, "Am I mature enough to collaborate?" We believe people who can truly collaborate are those who have acquired some level of generativity. Generativity is the stage in Erik Erikson's model of human development where an individual has the ability to move beyond self and to extend care and concern for others. In order to achieve this stage of development, a person must navigate the previous stages with a certain degree of success. Then a person possesses qualities that are essential for collaboration.

For example, a person trusts others and has the capacity to work both independently and with others. There is present the ability to take initiative and try new things without an inordinate fear of failure, as well as a healthy independence. There is recognition of the value of working cooperatively with others and an absence of over-competitiveness that frees the person to engage in situations that require "give and take." Generative people are not overly consumed with self interest, but can extend themselves to others. They have a clear sense of their own identity and are able to relate to others at a level of intimacy. It is clear that the qualities describing a generative person are those same qualities necessary for collaborative ministry. While no one is completely mature in every aspect of development, an individual must possess a sufficient level of psycho-sexual development in order to collaborate effectively.

Conclusion

The first step in implementing collaborative ministry is to assess the present level at which the group is operating: co-existence, communication, cooperation, or true collaboration. This is followed by the decision to attend to the "Four C's" of collaboration: clarification, conviction, commitment, capacity, and capability.

Reflection/Discussion Questions

1. Which of the four levels of collaboration most clearly describes and characterizes us?
2. What is our agreed upon basic definition of collaboration?
3. Why are we convinced that we need to function more collaboratively?
4. What are the major obstacles and fears which prevent us from being more committed? Are we willing not only to identify them, but also to discuss them? What steps do I, personally, need to take to overcome these obstacles and fears, and am I willing to do what is required?
5. Which skills do we need to develop? How will we do that?
6. What are my fears of sharing faith? When will we share faith?
7. When will we discern gifts? What process will be used?
8. What can I do to attend to my own personal development? How can I create a climate which is conducive to helping each person develop psycho-sexually?
9. What am I personally planning to do in order to become more collaborative?

2

Myths of Collaborative Ministry

As collaborative ministry grows in popularity, so too does the number of myths and misconceptions about it. This chapter highlights some of the more common myths and misconceptions. While some myths have negligible effect on the collaborative effort, others, left unexamined, can wreak havoc on a collaborative venture. Seven common myths are discussed in this chapter.

Table 2.1

Common Myths About Collaboration
1. Collaboration is easy.
2. Membership in a group constitutes collaboration.
3. Collaboration is an end in itself.
4. Collaboration is primarily about decision-making, power, and authority.
5. Consensus is the only appropriate decision-making process in a collaborative group.
6. Collaboration is egalitarian. There is no place for a designated leader.
7. Collaboration is limited to staff/team.

Myth #1—Collaboration Is Easy

While the concept of collaboration is simple and straightforward, the implementation is more complicated than it first appears. *Collaboration is not easy.* It demands working closely, often intimately and intensely, with others. By its very nature collaborative ministry is relational. In the midst of relating to others, anger, hostility, and conflict inevitably erupt.

Collaboration requires effort on the part of all involved. Desire for collaboration is a good starting point, but desire alone is insufficient for a successful endeavor. The desire must be accompanied by a willingness to invest time, energy, and one's self if collaboration is to succeed.

Collaboration demands good communication in general. In particular, the communication must be around a common understanding of collaboration and must occur in the early stages. If everyone is working from a different understanding of collaboration, the result will inevitably be frustration and chaos. For example, when a person's behavior does not meet my expectations I become frustrated and my frustration is one of the trigger points of anger. I become angry when my co-worker does not meet my expectations; anger is a pre-condition for conflict.

Conflict is difficult and uncomfortable for most Christians. If the conflict is not addressed, tension will emerge and will not evaporate merely with the passage of time. This ever-present tension often leads to the breakdown of collaborative efforts. The chain of events generated by the differing percep-tions points out why collaborative ministry is not easy. In addition, it is sometimes messy because we are dealing with other fallible human beings like ourselves. Thus, collaboration is far from simple. It is difficult and demands a strong com-mitment based on beliefs about mission and gospel.

Myth #2—Membership in a Group Constitutes Collaboration

The second myth is that merely working with others in ministry constitutes collaboration. Membership in a particular ministry, be that on a parish team, school faculty, hospital staff, campus ministry team, or diocesan staff, does not constitute, *ipso facto*, collaborative ministry. Collaborative ministry involves an intentional and conscious decision to minister in that manner, and it is distinguished by certain characteristics like those represented in Table 2.2.

	Characteristics of Collaborative Ministry
Table 2.2	• There is a common and explicit vision. • Ministry is based on gift. • There is a respect of others' gifts. • Collaborative ministry responds to a human need. • There is an ongoing search for ways to call forth the gifts in the larger Christian community.

Collaborative ministry is always oriented toward mission. Groups that are collaborating should have a *common and explicit vision* that is mission-oriented. This vision must be discussed, negotiated, articulated, and shared by the group. It should be a vision which is capable of moving the group beyond itself to respond to needs in the wider community. The Old Testament prophets caution that when there is no vision the people perish. When the vision lacks a specific mission dimension, the group frequently becomes self-serving and narcissistic.

One of the distinguishing aspects of true collaborative ministry is that it is *based on gift*. Any group that wishes to minister collaboratively must seriously engage in an ongoing process of gift discernment and acquire mechanisms to fully employ those gifts in a common mission.

Collaborative ministry involves not only the recognition of the gifts of others, but also an *affirmation and respect of those gifts*. This can be a real area of challenge, for it is not always easy to affirm the gifts of other people, especially the gifts that are most different from one's own. Our experience has shown that it is this lack of mutual respect which often erodes collaborative efforts. More than once we have been asked, "What can we do with person X?" Our response is always the same, "What gifts do you see in X?" The climate for collaboration begins to blossom when the individuals who pose the question can perceive the other as a gifted person and can enumerate the many and varied gifts possessed by him or her. When this new view is taken, one's perspective changes. "I never thought about her or him that way!" is a common response. When one can recognize, respect, and cherish the gifts and person of another, then the potential for collaboration becomes maximized.

The opposite is also true. It is extremely difficult to collaborate with someone whose gifts one cannot recognize or respect. During a program we asked for a volunteer to share his gifts with the group. As one man volunteered another man spontaneously muttered a mild expletive. During a break we asked the spontaneous responder the reason for his response. He answered, "Of all the people in this group to volunteer, he is the only one in whom I can't see any gifts." When the others enumerated the gifts of the volunteer, we invited him to sit back and observe and ask himself why he was unable to identify any gifts in that person. Until he could respect his co-worker's gifts, he would be unable to engage in collaboration with the person.

All ministry responds to a human need. Ministry that is collaborative searches for ways to match differing gifts with the numerous human and societal needs present in our world.

On occasion groups direct their energy almost exclusively to developing collaboration within the core group itself. Their goal is not an ever-expanding attempt to *identify and release the gifts of others.* Rather, the focus of collaboration is limited to building a sense of corporate unity.

Through baptism every Christian is called to ministry; it is both a right and a privilege. The focus of collaborative ministry is to empower and animate the entire Christian community to respond to their baptismal call by using their God-given gifts in ministry and service. The goal of collaborative ministry is always the incorporation of 100 percent of the gifts. The primary role of Christian leaders is animating the people of God, and facilitating their response to the call to ministry.

Myth #3—Collaboration Is an End in Itself

As groups discuss and implement collaborative ministry, it is easy to get caught up in the dynamics and details, and lose sight of the true purpose. Groups can expend all their energy exclusively in developing a collaborative climate among themselves. Those working collaboratively have to challenge themselves to always keep in sight the ultimate end of any collaborative effort, i.e., animating the gifts of the entire people of God and furthering the mission of Christ.

Myth #4—Collaboration Is Primarily About Decision-Making, Power, and Authority

When listening to groups discuss collaborative ministry the emphasis of the conversation can quickly shift from ministry and escalate into a heated debate about power and authority. In fact, in some situations competing and vying for power and authority has become the primary focus. Ministry is not about power. It is about service. The power which should concern a collaborative group is the unleashing of the *power of gifts* to meet the pressing unmet needs in our world. This is not to diminish the real issue of power and powerlessness that can be endemic in the church. Rather, it is an attempt to invite each person to look at one's own motivating force. At times obsession with the issue of power can be a form of resistance and defensiveness against the commitment to ministry.

Myth #5—Consensus Is the Only Appropriate Decision-Making Process

Consensus seems to have been elevated to the status of a God-given, gospel form of decision-making. Many in the church seem to make consensus the eleventh commandment. Perhaps this myth emerged out of a belief that "good" Christians should not engage in conflict. Striving valiantly to avoid conflict can stagnate a group. Sometimes mature engagement in conflict produces the most Christ-like results.

The myth of consensus seems to have a strong foothold in the church, for example in guidelines that are being developed for parish pastoral councils in many dioceses. As we expressed in *Building Christian Community*, there are times when consensus is both the most appropriate and most effective form of decision-making. Likewise, there are countless times when it is neither the most effective, nor the most appropriate form.

Ultimately, the form of decision-making adopted should be chosen because of the conviction that it is the method which will be most conducive in discerning and implementing God's will.

Collaboration does not mean homogenization. It is not imperative for everyone to agree or think alike. Nor is it essential to find a solution with which everyone is comfortable or with which everyone can live. Not everyone can live with what the gospel demands. Living one's Christianity is sometimes very uncomfortable.

Myth #6—Collaboration Is Egalitarian

The myth that leadership ceases in a collaborative model is all too commonly held. Thus a group attempts to develop an egalitarian structure in which no individual has the authority to make decisions or to call others to accountability. In our experience, leaderless groups do not function to their maximum capacity.

The basic premise of collaboration is that there are many gifts in any Christian community, and each gift has a value and a place. There are no greater or lesser gifts, as St. Paul reminds us, only different ones (1 Cor 12:4). Leadership is a gift and, like any other gift, it should be affirmed and joined with other gifts to further the reign of God. Too frequently, collaborative efforts fail because the group is unwilling to allow anyone to utilize the gift of leadership.

Myth #7—Collaboration Is Limited to Staff or Team

When we first began conducting workshops on collaboration there was a pervading myth that collaboration was only for members of the staff (e.g., parish or diocesan). Although there are still places where this myth remains, there has been movement in the fuller understanding of collaborative ministry. Over the intervening years, the focus for collaboration has shifted from the staff to the larger organization itself: the diocese, the parish, the school. Now as development continues the question becomes, "How do we collaborate between and among units?" This is a clear indication of the growth that is occurring. What is the next level of development for collaborative ministry? Our hypothesis is that there will be a greater ecumenical collaboration, and collaboration between church organizations and civic organizations.

Table 2.3	*Evolution of Collaborative Focus* 1. Focus on the staff, team, or faculty. 2. Focus on 100 percent of the people in the larger unit (parish, school, diocese). 3. Focus between units (departments, parishes in a region, schools). 4. Focus on interdisciplinary, ecumenical, other agencies, civic, etc.

Conclusion

Any innovative or new idea is fertile ground for mythology to germinate. This is particularly true when there is a certain amount of ambiguity about the concept. Given the ambiguity which did and may still exist about collaboration, it is not surprising that myths have developed. We encourage the reader to explore the myths of collaborative ministry which might be part of your individual or collective belief systems. With a group, surface some myths held by your group. Create a safe climate within the group where these myths can be explored and discussed. If possible, allow the differences and conflicts to emerge so that new insights can be achieved.

This chapter has highlighted some of the myths which are prevalent in many groups. Though you may not agree with our assessment, we would encourage you, and your group, to discuss these myths.

Reflection/Discussion Questions

1. Which of the myths listed in this chapter have I held or do I hold? Do I disagree with any of the myths? Why is this so?
2. What are additional myths which exist that would be valuable for us to discuss?

3. Reflect on your own attempts at collaboration. Where has it been difficult? What made it easier? How effective is your communication? As a group do you possess a common understanding of collaboration? Have you arrived at a common understanding through discussion or is it simply an assumption?

4. As you read and reflect on the five characteristics (Table 2.2) that describe collaborative ministry, do you agree with them? Are there others you would add? Are these the characteristics which describe your collaborative efforts?

3

Evolution of Collaborative Ministry

"Isn't It Time to Put the Power of Shared Leadership to Work for You?"

This question was emblazoned as a full page advertisement in *USA Today* announcing a leadership series to be held in New York. The featured speakers were the proclaimed major gurus in the leadership field including: Peter Drucker, Tom Peters, Stephen Covey, Rosabeth Moss Kanter, Ken Blanchard, and Peter Senge.

This evolving appreciation and valuing of shared leadership is not a new phenomenon. Regularly, advertisements appear in daily newspapers extolling some new book that espouses a "breakthrough" in leadership and management techniques for the corporate world. Among the many such books, one that caught our attention was *The Death of Competition* by James F. Moore. The advertisement for the book read in part:

> In business today, innovation wins. But you can't create the future alone. You must gather allies. You must coevolve with others in your ecosystem: customers, suppliers, employees, investors and communities—and even sometimes your competitors.

It doesn't take a great deal of imagination to translate this business language into ecclesial language. Isn't it time for the church to consider putting the power of shared leadership to use in effectively carrying out its divine mission? What can the church learn from the business field? Though there is much that the church can learn, in this area of shared leadership, it is the church, not the business world that has been the innovator and leader. For decades through its ecclesial documents, the church has been inviting its members to shared leadership, which is usually described as "collaborative ministry."

The business world and the church have much to learn from each other. They each bring to the table gifts and insights to influence the other. Cardinal Mahony attests to this reality:

> The ministers of the church will have much to learn from the skills of collaboration developed in business, education, and other arenas of life. Leaders in these realms of life should have much to learn from the Church community about the deeper communion of life we all share and the sacred quality of all persons (PAL).

Over the last few decades church documents from the Vatican, National and State Bishops' Conferences, and from individual bishops have encouraged collaboration, collaborative ministry, and collaborative leadership. The desire and concern for greater collaboration is not limited to the hierarchy but echoes in almost any gathering of committed Christians seeking to discover more faithful and effective ways of continuing the mission of Jesus Christ.

This clarion call to collaborative ministry is stated succinctly by Pope John Paul II, in his address to the Bishops' Conference of France during their 1997 *ad limina* visit: "To guide and enliven pastoral units, the collaboration of priests and lay persons is increasingly necessary" (ALA).

Similarly, in 1990 the USCCB defined this evolving concept of collaboration as "the working together of all the baptized, each contributing specific, personal gifts" (GU, p. 49). Eight years later this same conference acknowledged that collaboration is indeed a "huge task," indicated some "practical steps to promote it," and raised some primary questions to be addressed by anyone involved in collaboration:

> First, we need to examine our own beliefs and behaviors and confront those that may hinder our ability to collaborate. Do we see collaboration as a genuine value, in which we invest time and energy? Collaboration can promote joint ownership of the mission, but it does require more

time. What strengths and weaknesses do we bring? Are we willing to trust others, or do we have an excessive need for control? (FWD, p. 19).

In case there is any doubt, they remind us that, "no one is the perfect collaborator" (FWD, p. 19) but ultimately, "collaboration is a means for becoming who God wants us to be" (FWD, p. 21). Collaboration is a response to God's invitation and call. The evolution of the understanding of collaborative ministry could be compared to a cloudy morning when the rising sun dispels the fog and the day gradually becomes clearer. Each new ecclesial document casts greater clarity, consistency, and richness on this evolving concept. This emerging clarity comes through in a series of documents promulgated by the USCCB. One such prophetic document, *Called and Gifted for the Third Millennium*, reminds all Christians of their call to holiness, community, mission and ministry, and Christian maturity. It concludes by revealing that growth in all areas will occur when Christians embrace the call to be more collaborative. The document also clearly indicates that the proposed model is based on the concept of giftedness:

> The Church's pastoral ministry can be more effective if we become true collaborators, mindful of our weaknesses, but grateful for our gifts. Collaboration challenges us to understand that we are, in reality, joined in Christ's body, that we are not separate but interdependent (CG, p. 24).

Principles of Collaboration

The call to collaborative ministry is a call to personal and communal conversion. Anyone who wishes to become collaborative must surrender herself or himself to God. The surrender involves a refining and conversion that allows God to take control over one's life. Collaboration is not easy. It requires a radical letting go. It exemplifies the process of death-resurrection:

> Collaborative ministry begins from a fundamental desire to work together because we are called by the Lord to be a company of disciples, not isolated individuals. It grows through a mutual process of conversion and formation (SWG, p. 17).

Five principles of collaboration emerge from the documents we have studied. They are listed in Table 3.1 and summarized in the following sections.

Table 3.1	*Key Principles of Collaborative Ministry*
	1. There is a universal call to ministry.
	2. The call to collaborative ministry is based on the concept of gift.
	3. The goal of collaborative ministry is a call to mission, to evangelization, and to the transformation of the world.
	4. There is a developing theological rationale for fostering collaborative ministry.

Universal Call to Ministry

Our concept of collaborative ministry is predicated on the belief that 100 percent of all baptized Christians are called to ministry. For the Christian, ministry is not a choice, but rather, a call, a privilege, and a responsibility. Numerous documents from the Vatican and the USCCB have directly referred to this universal call to ministry. Some examples follow.

The USCCB has explicitly reaffirmed this concept of the universal call to ministry. They call every Christian to "mission and ministry" (CG, p. 14f) and quote *Christifideles Laici* in proclaiming,

> . . . The Holy Spirit pours out gifts which make it possible for every Christian man and woman to assume different ministries and forms of service that complement one another and are for the good of all (CG, p. 15).

The United States Catholic Conference (USCC) in clear and unambiguous language speaks of the universal call to ministry in a commentary by the USCCB Committee on the Liturgy:

> Ministry is the privilege and responsibility of the total Church, and everyone is called by baptism to exercise it, each in his or her own way and according to his or her own call and gifts (MC, p. 20).

And, the document from the Committee on Women in Society and in the Church states:

> Collaboration in ministry has assumed new importance since the Second Vatican Council stressed that all the baptized are called to a life of holiness and service (FWD, p. 17).

In his *Pastoral Letter on the Role of the Laity in the Life of the Archdiocese of Los Angeles*, Roger Mahony frequently refers to the universal call to ministry: "God has called each one of you personally." (ROL, p. 4). A "calling," Mahony indicates, is a sharing in "the ministry of Jesus" (ROL, p. 6f). Referring to the *Decree on the Apostolate of the Laity*, Mahony adds, "that the Christian vocation is essentially *a vocation to ministry*" (p. 6) and reminds us that the Second Vatican Council describes this ministry as being "indispensable" (p. 6). Cardinal Mahony affirms this broad definition of ministry. He writes that there are laity,

> who exercise a form of "ministry" in their families, work places, and local communities . . . we all can and must minister to one another . . . there are innumerable ministries that require no further authentication than our Baptism (cf. Gal 3:23-29; PAL p. 15f).

The development of the universal call to ministry is occurring in places other than the United States. The Archdiocese of Brisbane, as mentioned earlier, has produced several documents as part of a pastoral planning process. The Brisbane documents develop a rationale for the universal call that begins with the conviction that baptism is the primary source which calls for all to participate in God's mission. They further indicate in a seminal document which gave form to their pastoral planning that,

> all the baptized are called into the mission of Christ, within and beyond the church, according to the gifts they have received and the needs discovered in their communities. Some exercise ministry in the church. But ALL are called to express God's compassion and service in the wider world (SOF).

Some documents have restricted the term minister to the ordained. There is a universal call to place one's gifts at the service of the gospel. Whether this response will be called ministry or some other term is left for future development.

Giftedness

The essence and motivating force of collaborative ministry is the rich biblical concept of gift, expressed most forcefully and clearly in the writings of St. Paul. Collaboration is enhanced when the gifts of the entire people of God are identified and released in ministry and service in order to foster or extend the reign of God.

While the documents previously quoted in this chapter emphasize the intimate relationship between giftedness and collaborative ministry, the USCCB document on women in the church has the most complete and expansive description of collaborative ministry. For example, it states:

> An appreciation of gifts—our own and those of others—is crucial. The Second Vatican Council teaches that the Spirit gives different gifts for the well-being of the church and that all believers have the "right and duty to use them (their gifts) in the church and in the world for the good of humanity and the development of the Church" (AA, #3). Collaborative ministry is rooted in baptism, based on the gifts of each believer, and connected to the mission of the church and to its nature as *communio* (FWD, p. 18).

Reflecting on women's experiences, the bishops indicate the harm that is done when gifts (both women's and men's) are not appreciated, valued, and utilized:

> We have heard women speak of their satisfaction when ordained leaders recognize their gifts and skills and use them to serve the church's mission. We have also heard women speak of their hurt and pain when ordained leaders reject or do not fully use these gifts (FWD, p. 6).

The bishops emphasize the responsibility to overcome and eliminate anything which interferes with the full utilization of gifts.

Pastors are challenged to use their power to evoke the gifts of others and to strive to eliminate the obstacles that prevent the full use of those gifts (FWD, p. 19).

We reiterate that placing an emphasis on the relationship between collaboration and giftedness is not limited to the United States. The Bishops' Conference of England and Wales stress the need for collaboration. For example:

Involvement in collaborative ministry . . . calls us to work together on equal terms; the conviction that our different gifts are complementary and mutually enriching; an agreement that we are accountable to each other for how we work and what we do (SWG, p. 17).

The rationale for collaborative ministry flows from the universal call to ministry and the baptismal theology which speaks of the giftedness and call of every baptized person. The direction in which those gifts are being called collaboratively leads to the third key principle of collaborative ministry.

Mission Orientation

The goal of collaborative ministry is the same as the mission of Jesus Christ, i.e., to extend the reign of God. As Cardinal Mahony stated: "The church is called to serve the world, not itself" (ROL, p. 7). Resistance occurs when mission-oriented people encounter individuals and groups who view collaborative ministry as an end in itself, devoid of a mission orientation.

Collaborative ministry never exists for its own sake. Some pseudo-collaborative projects tend to project an image of narcissism. The sole purpose of collaborative ministry is to foster the mission of Jesus Christ and to create the conditions which allow for the coming of the reign of God. In true collaboration the group's energy is expended in fostering and advancing an aspect of Christ's mission. Ultimately, the major criteria by which any group assesses its success or growth as a collaborative endeavor is the degree to which it is successful in carrying out the divine mission.

The Second Vatican Council taught that the church has but one intention, namely, "that the Kingdom of God may come and salvation of the human race may be accomplished" (CMW, #45). The essential relationship between mission and collaboration is best expressed by Pope John Paul II, who declared:

> To proclaim Jesus Christ in all cultures is the church's central concern and the object of its mission. In our time, it demands, first, that cultures be discerned as a human reality to be evangelized and, consequently, the pressing need for a new kind of collaboration among all those responsible for the work of evangelization (NE).

Many dioceses have made great strides in fostering this mission-oriented concept of collaborative ministry. The diocese of Albany, New York has chosen collaborative ministry as their "number one diocesan priority"(ELM). Bishop Hubbard, who is a leading proponent of collaborative ministry, is clear in proclaiming his own vision of mission:

> The church must always understand itself as not existing for itself but for the world. The church can never be a mission or ministry unto itself; rather, it is to be a community of ministers charged with the task of bringing the healing presence of Christ to a wounded humanity (NCP).

Bishops' conferences throughout the world also stress the relationship between mission and collaborative ministry. The recent pastorals by the bishops of England and Wales directly speak to this relationship:

> Collaborative ministry is ministry committed to mission. It is not simply concerned with the internal life of the church. Rather, it shows to the world the possibility of transformation, of community, and of unity within diversity (SWG, p. 17).

Likewise, the bishops of Latin America have commented in the same vein:

> We pledge to increase fraternity in the communities, encouraging interpersonal relations within them that will foster integration and will lead to greater communion and missionary collaboration (LAB).

The call of the church is to be an evangelizing church with a strong sense of mission. Furthermore, accomplishment of this mission requires a commitment to build a more collaborative church. A statement by the Catholic bishops of Florida summarizes this conviction:

> In the service of God one does not work alone but in collaboration with many others . . . Self-sufficient attitudes, individualism, the lack of mutual collaboration and inability to dialogue do not reflect the image of Christ and his message and result in ineffective ministry (PLL).

Theological Foundations

Collaboration is a theological concept, not merely a management or organizational principle. The theology of collaborative ministry is still in evolution. Pope Paul VI contextualized the theology of collaboration in the very act of the Incarnation:

> By pronouncing her "fiat" at the Annunciation and giving her consent to the Incarnation, Mary was already collaborating with the whole work her son was to accomplish (CPG, #15).

Presently, the theology of collaborative ministry is primarily focused on three theological concepts: Trinity, sacrament and *communio*.

Trinity

Some theologies of collaborative ministry have likened it to the Trinity—that is, separate persons constituting one God with one common mission. For example, the bishops of Florida state,

> Collaborative ministry reflects the life of the One, Triune God. It also reflects the mission of the church to be the link between God and human beings among themselves (PLL, p. 2).

Within the unity of the Trinity, it is the Holy Spirit who is most closely associated with the emerging theology of collaborative ministry: "To each individual the manifestation of the Spirit is given for some benefit" (1 Cor 12:7). Throughout his writings, St. Paul profoundly unwraps the mysteries of those manifestations or gifts.

Sacrament

The sacramental dimension of collaborative ministry, "is rooted in baptism, based on the gifts of each believer, and connected to the mission of the church and to its nature as *communio*" (FWD, p. 18).

Bishop Hubbard explained it in these words in *Fulfilling the Vision*:

> The first assumption is that the concept of shared responsibility and collaborative ministry, based upon the baptismal call that is given to each member of the church, must serve as a foundation for the church's efforts to advance the mission and ministry of Jesus in our world.

However, the recent document of the bishops of England and Wales has broadened the sacramental understanding of collaborative ministry beyond just baptism:

> Collaborative ministry brings together into partnership people who, through baptism and confirmation, as well as ordination and marriage, have different vocations, gifts, and offices within the church. It does not blur the distinctiveness of each vocation or gift. Rather it enables the identity of each to be seen and expressed more fully (SWG, p. 17).

Communio

As was noted before, the Document on Women describes the nature of the church as *communio* (community in a deep and profound sense). Communio demands an acknowledgment by each Christian of one's God-given gifts and an acceptance of those gifts on the part of the community. The document *From Words to Deeds* points out that

> these charisms build up the entire body of Christ and "are to be accepted with gratitude by the person who receives them and by all members of the Church as well" (FWD, p. 8 quoting CCC #3).

Archbishop William Borders describes the entire church as a "community of collaborative ministries." Borders states:

> Before any distinction of roles or offices in the church, we stand as one family of the baptized. It is the community as a whole to whom is given the primary responsibility for the mission of the church, and it is the whole community which stands as the first minister of the kingdom (RP).

Education and Collaboration

The focus of this chapter has been on ecclesial documents and their role in helping to clarify and to direct collaborative ministry. However, the bishops are not alone in this undertaking. Educational institutions and organizations are giving increased attention to collaborative ministry. For example, the Congregation of Christian Education in Rome has challenged school communities around the world to become more collaborative as evidenced by the following statement:

> The more the members of the educational community develop a real willingness to collaborate among themselves, the more fruitful their work will be (RDE).

The Congregation also suggests that "misunderstanding and various tensions" which emerge in the daily life of a school can be overcome by developing a "determination to collaborate."

The determination to collaborate has influenced the attitudes and directions taken by Catholic educators around the world. The Second Vatican Council challenged schools to become a "community in which the various gifts of the people of God are respected and enhanced for the good of the community as a whole" (CMW). Canadian Catholic schools are directed "to actively build collaborative school communities, and they are to develop the skills of working with others, especially given Canada's diverse population" (CCS).

In the United States, the National Catholic Education Association encourages its members to develop collaboration and collaborative leadership. The document *Those Who Hear You Hear Me: A Resource for Bishops and Diocesan Educational/Catechetical Leaders* points out that

> [e]ach ministry can be fully realized only when these ministries share a common vision and act upon this vision together with the other ministries. It is a powerful and dynamic concept. Too often, its potential is limited to the conceptual level, and sometimes fails to energize the mission (TWH, p. 2).

The document also states that "collaboration ensure(s) vitality for the whole" (p. 4) and challenges leaders to become more collaborative for the sake of the students they are serving:

> The support for the entire mission will call leaders to collaborate across every area of our mission and at every level. Our leaders will call for shared vision rather than isolated perspectives; collaboration rather than competition; mutual support rather than comparisons. Leaders will be prepared to minister in the midst of slow change, and even resistance (TWH, p. 4).

The document states an apt conclusion, that "the very foundation of hope is the collaborative ministry of total Catholic education" (TWH, p. 4).

Conclusion

Ecclesial and other church leaders have, in many different ways, spoken compellingly about the need for collaborative ministry. Their pronouncements give form, shape, and substance to the concept of collaborative ministry. The rhetoric is forceful. What remains is for all the people of God, including the ecclesial leaders, to activate the words in a more intentional and committed fashion.

Reflection/Discussion Questions

1. How is my understanding of collaborative ministry different than it was ten years ago? What has influenced this change?
2. What would I identify as the key principles of collaborative ministry?
3. How am I being called to translate the words into action?

4

Obstacles to Collaborative Ministry

The development of a model of collaborative ministry starts with clarification of the term. Since the word "collaboration" may convey different meanings, taking time to come to a common understanding of the word is an important initial activity.

Once the group arrives at a common agreement on the concept of collaboration, they can explore their convictions in the value of collaboration. It is important that the group believe that collaboration is worth the time, energy, and potential stress involved. Unless there is a strong conviction among the participants, the collaborative enterprise, like the seed described in the gospels of Matthew (13:4-23) and Mark (4:1-20), will be devoured by hungry birds, scorched by the broiling sun, or choked by weeds.

In our experience the first two steps of the "4C" process—clarifying the meaning of collaboration and identifying reasons why people are convinced of its need—are relatively easy. Ideally, these steps should consume a minimum of time. This is not true for the third C, commitment. Commitment is the pivotal area which ultimately determines the success or failure of a collaborative enterprise. Commitment involves identifying and addressing the obstacles that prevent a total, unreserved dedication to the collaborative effort.

The last few years we have focused the bulk of our workshop time identifying and dealing with the obstacles. This approach emphasizes our belief that attending to one's personal obstacles is the area most likely to be resisted. It is also the area which, when addressed, provides the greatest growth in commitment to collaborative ministry.

If asked to identify obstacles to collaborative ministry, most people tend to focus on other people. It is more comfortable to focus on obstacles outside self than on those which are internal and in need of personal growth and conversion. Edwin Friedman, the systems therapist and analyst, proposed that the secret to motivating others is to spend time in "self-definition," that is, analyzing those areas of self which are in need of change.

This approach does not deny the reality that there are a myriad of systemic and institutional obstacles. Nor does it minimize the reality that those with whom we minister are in need of change and conversion.

In Bishop Anthony Pilla's final address as president of the USCCB in 1998, he alluded to one of the institutional obstacles, power:

> Unfortunately, some interpret the council's vision, which was meant to bring about a sense of closer communion and collaboration among the members of the church, as simply a shift in the power structure of an organization (RRL).

It is an indisputable reality that issues such as the misuse of power and the "isms" which cry out for vengeance are as much a reality in the church as they are in the wider society. Too frequently the church is guilty of reflecting society, rather than assuming its prophetic stance, that of witnessing the radical dimension of the gospel. This is true both for the institutional church and for the church as the people of God. There will be greater success in collaboration when all involved expend more energy addressing the obstacles in themselves.

Table 4.1 lists some of the more prevalent obstacles. The text material that follows offers more detail about each obstacle. At the end of the chapter you will be invited to add additional obstacles based on your experience.

Table 4.1	*The Major Obstacles to Collaborative Ministry* • low self-esteem • arrogance and self-righteousness • burnout • hostility • failure to deal with conflict • lack of forgiveness • failure to deal with loss • lack of knowledge of gifts • failure to share faith • lack of an integrated sexuality • learned helplessness

Self-Esteem

Self-esteem was not initially apparent as the predominate obstacle to collaborative ministry. Though low self-esteem seemed to be present in many of the previously listed obstacles (e.g., *Collaborative Ministry: Skills and Guidelines*, Chapter 2), its overriding importance gradually became more clear.

Over the years in workshop experiences, participants would name behavior-related obstacles such as competition, parochialism, and the like. Upon further examination these behaviors are indicative of a more primal cause. All behavior is need-directed. Behavior is only a facade for masking the real obstacle, the unmet or threatened needs. In order to unearth the true obstacle we had to urge people to look beyond their behavior in order to determine what influenced their action. What surfaced repeatedly was the issue of self-esteem. The document on women, cited earlier, also makes this direct connection between low self-esteem and behavior that militates against collaboration:

> Personal traits, as well as education and life experiences affect our ability to collaborate. An example is low self-esteem, which can produce the hostility and competitiveness that work against collaboration (FWD, p. 19).

One expression of low self-esteem is inordinate competitiveness. We live in a world that fosters, values, and rewards competitiveness. A spirit of competition can stimulate a person to explore new expressions of creativity and to unfold new avenues of growth and human potential. Competition among teams, for example, also illustrates the necessity for working together with others, and for combining talents and gifts most effectively in reaching a goal. However, some people develop an ordinate destructive competitiveness that blinds them to the gifts of others and interferes with their freedom to unite their gifts with others in ministry.

Competitiveness appears to be endemic in many places in our world today. It is even praised as a distinguishing trait of American culture. An article in an airline magazine shockingly extolled excessive United States competition at the expense of developing nations, complaining that although the United States still has the strongest economy in the world, developing nations threaten the high standard of living we've come to take for granted. The solution proposed was "a comprehensive national commitment to competitiveness."

An excessively competitive culture creates an obstacle to collaboration. Competitiveness is present in the church as overly competitive individuals, in a competitive culture, are asked to participate collaboratively as adult Christians in ministry. This overly-competitive attitude is the antithesis of collaboration.

The emphasis on perfection that characterized the church in the past has presumably contributed to a lowered sense of self-esteem which produces excessively competitive behavior (*Design for Wholeness*, pp. 81-109). When self-esteem is tied to success, and success is equated with perfection, the results are disastrous. This attitude inevitably creates problems when individuals are forced to confront their humanness and lack of perfection. They adopt some form of compensatory behavior to counteract the lowered self-esteem.

The method of compensation can take different avenues of expression. For some, the stark realization that they will never be perfect can trigger depression; for others, cynicism. Some will compensate with the fight/flight reaction, either becoming exceedingly belligerent or giving up completely. Others will settle for survival: "I think I can hold on for another year." Their experience of life is no longer one of continued Christian growth and challenge, but one of stagnation.

One of the more destructive reactions to this diminish-ment of self-esteem is to attempt to rebuild self-esteem by devaluing others. We visited an egalitarian society in which certain persons were described as "knockers." Any individual who began to stand out or rise above the others was immedi-ately "knocked down." Ministers who possess a low self-esteem can become knockers. Belittling is the opposite of affirming and it impedes collaboration.

Destructive competitiveness and knocking occurs between groups as well as among individuals. Competition between groups is most intense when the self-esteem of group members is based more on the qualities and accomplishments of the group than on the self. In religious congregations, for example, the unique spirit and charism which characterizes the congre-gation can subtly become the basis for comparison and rivalry with other congregations. Teaching communities can begin comparing themselves with other teaching communities and can convince themselves that they are the best educators in the diocese. This can result in a condescending, arrogant attitude toward the other congregations. Or, a congregation that choos-es a specific apostolate, for example, a center for battered wives, can believe that their group is more relevant and impor-tant than the other congregations involved in more traditional ministries. We have observed communities which boast about how superior they are to other communities because they not only work with the poor, but also live among them. While at times competitiveness is subtle, it sometimes becomes quite blatant. Whatever form it takes, it has deleterious effects on collaboration.

A similar attitude can develop on a parish or school level, when healthy pride in the institution degenerates into an atti-tude of "our parish/school is better than your parish/school." Within the parish or school, petty squabbles may arise between organizations. Whenever an overly com-petitive attitude dominates, whether at the individual, parish, congregation, or diocesan level, attempts at collabora-tion will be virtually impossible.

Another way in which low self-esteem can manifest itself is through an attitude of *parochialism*. Parochialism is charac-terized by narrowness of thinking. It often leads to an attitude of exclusive concern for one group with a corresponding apathy toward anyone not of that group. Unfortunately, in many ministerial situations vision can become limited to "my parish," "our school or hospital," or "my diocese." Since the thrust of Christianity is evangelization, not maintenance, parochial vision is contrary to the goal of Christianity. The gifts and talents of individuals or groups are given by God for extending the kingdom, both in their immediate sphere and in the wider church.

A pastor in the Philippines described the collaboration and cooperation between his parish and a neighboring one, which had twice as many parishioners. He characterized both parishes as vital Christian communities and attributed the parishes' vitality to lay leadership and collaboration between the two parishes. As he spoke, it became clear that lay leadership had been fostered and laity were now responsible for almost all the ministry occurring within the parishes. Also, the two parishes worked together whenever a need was identified. For instance, if someone worked well with youth in one parish, that person organized the youth program for the area, regardless of parish boundaries. If someone had a gift for marriage preparation programs, that person conducted the programs in both parishes. It was evident that the pastors of both parishes had a high level of self-esteem, which permitted them to eschew both competition and parochialism.

While low self-esteem is the major obstacle, it is also one of the more difficult obstacles to overcome. Ultimately, no one can give or take self-esteem from another. Each individual must take personal responsibility for his or her level of self-esteem. Although no one can give self-esteem, one can create a climate that fosters and contributes to building or maintaining self-esteem. One way to create a climate is a gift discernment process, where a person is presented with the positive qualities that others have observed.

Arrogance and Self-Righteousness

Collaboration is unlikely to occur if individuals approach one another from a stance of superiority. Arrogance and self-righteousness blind people to the gifts of others. Arrogance is one of the most difficult and pernicious obstacles to overcome because it remains hidden to those who possess it. We refer to arrogance and self-righteousness as a "diabolical" obstacle. Solutions can be identified to overcome other obstacles, but this one seems immune to change. One reason is because arrogant and self-righteous people are unaware of their affliction. Arrogant people are not attracted to collaboration because they don't see the need for the gifts of anyone else. Perceiving themselves as the storehouse of all knowledge, wisdom, and giftedness, they are convinced that if everyone else would listen to them everything would work fine.

Arrogance can affect anyone in ministry. People in positions of authority may perceive themselves as superior to those they lead. Presumably they have been elected or chosen because their leadership gifts and abilities have been recognized and called forth. It is important for leaders to remember that leadership gifts and abilities are not superior to other gifts, only different.

On the other hand, people who feel stereotyped or victimized by those in leadership may compensate by assuming a posture of arrogance, often becoming extremely aggressive and vocal in denigrating those in leadership. They may perceive themselves as better qualified and more knowledgeable than the designated leadership.

We have witnessed countless situations in which clergy and religious have conveyed an attitude of superiority and arrogance toward the laity by presuming that they had much to teach the laity with little to learn from them. In reaction to this attitude, we have begun to observe some laity who presume that they are better qualified for some ministries than the clergy and religious, simply because they are laity. Both cases exemplify arrogance.

Arrogance is virtually impossible to perceive in oneself. Everyone needs the feedback of others to arrive at fuller self-knowledge. One test of a person's desire to achieve self-knowledge is the willingness to seek out honest feedback from others, especially when the feedback may be contrary with one's perception of himself or herself.

Arrogance and self-righteousness are related to low-self esteem. Like competition and parochialism, arrogance may also spring from the need to protect self-esteem, especially a fragile one. When a person feels inferior or insecure, adopting an attitude which conveys the opposite, one of superiority, can serve as a defense. Regardless of the cause, arrogance is destructive to collaboration.

Burnout

In the last few years we have observed an enthusiastic response to any presentation on burnout. Many people in ministry: laity, clergy, and religious, who are functioning in diverse roles and ministries, describe themselves as "burned out."

One of the difficulties about burnout is the vagueness of its definition. Burnout does not appear in the *Diagnostic and Statistic Manual IV*, making it a malady difficult to describe or diagnose. Though defying accurate description, so-called burnout still exists both as a painful reality and a major obstacle to collaborative ministry. Burnout is an obstacle for two reasons:

1. those who experience burnout lack the energy and/or interest to engage in collaborative ministry, and;
2. burned out individuals do not attract others to work with them nor do they encourage people who are seeking the Lord's promise of life (Jn 10:10) to follow them.

A review of the types of persons who are vulnerable to burnout can aid in personal reflection. In a comprehensive and informative article on burnout—"Burnout: A Growing Threat in Ministry"—Jesuit psychiatrist James Gill identifies potential candidates for burnout. He describes them as those who:

— work exclusively with distressed persons;
— work intensively with demanding people who feel entitled to assistance in solving their personal problems;
— are charged with the responsibility for too many individuals;
— feel strongly motivated to work with people but who are prevented from doing so by too many paperwork tasks;
— are perfectionists and thereby invite failure;

— cannot tolerate variety, novelty, or diversion in their work life;

— lack criteria for measuring the success of their undertakings but who experience an intense need to know they are doing a good job.

Burnout is the result of unrealistic expectations of self, rather than the amount of work. Unrealistic expectations, if linked with one's personal worth, can destroy a person. Unfortunately, most expectations are not conscious. It often takes the assistance of a friend, counselor, spiritual director, or supportive group to unearth and expunge these expectations from the recesses of the unconscious.

The movement from being a person who is energetic and enthusiastic to one who is tired and burned out does not occur in a single step. Burnout is a gradual, developmental process. Dr. James Tooley, of Mobile, Alabama, in an unpublished report, has identified four stages through which a person proceeds toward burnout:

Stage One—Obsession with One's Ministry

The initial phase of burnout is marked by an almost excessive, exclusive and obsessive commitment to one's work or ministry. The actual amount of work is not as much a factor as the attitudes and beliefs that drive the person, for example, that a good minister:

- is one who has no needs;
- is one who is always busy yet always available;
- is capable of being all things to all people at all times;
- knows that idle hands are the devil's workshop;
- has no time for or interest in developing any relationships;
- has answers to all the perplexing and inexplicable questions in life.

Internalizing such a set of beliefs creates unrealistic expectations that lead to an absorption with ministry to the exclusion of other aspects of life. An inability to set limits usually follows. Little or no time is allowed for recreation, friendships, or leisure activities. In short, those in the first stage of burnout become one-dimensional people who are obsessively committed to their ministry. Two descriptions characterize individuals at this stage: they are boring and they are sad. They are boring because their unbalanced life leaves them capable of talking only about their ministry. The sadness comes as a result of leading a one-dimensional, uninteresting life. When you encounter someone at this first stage, there is a desire to scream, "Get a life." One group recounted a meeting where someone commented on the sadness which seemed to pervade the whole atmosphere. After considering the comment they decided to do something about it. They printed a large banner proclaiming, "Fix Your Face!"

Stage Two—Exhaustion and Questioning

Persons in the second stage of burnout could be described as exhausted and questioning. It is possible to fairly accurately predict the dialogue of two people at this stage. One will declare their tiredness and the other will respond, "You think you are tired. Let me tell you how tired I am." For them, effectiveness in ministry is measured by how tired they feel.

The second characteristic of this stage is the questioning of many of the values that have sustained them throughout their personal and ministerial life. They would probably give voice to such questions as:
- What am I doing with my life?
- What difference am I making anyway?
- Is it really worth all the effort?

Stage Three—Withdrawal and Disappointment

The effect of these first two stages of burnout on collaboration is apparent. The invitation to minister with someone whose life conveys sadness and exhaustion is hardly attractive to healthy individuals. Such people tend to repel potential ministers rather than attract them. In addition, those experiencing constant exhaustion lack the energy to engage in anything beyond normal individual activities.

Burnout is actually depression, and in the third stage, in which a person withdraws from others and displays disappointment in self, others and ministry, this depression becomes more evident. Those experiencing the first two phases of burnout can reverse the downward spiral, usually with the support and challenge of friends or peers. However, in the third stage they avoid others and are no longer visible at community, parish, or staff functions. Stage 3 burnout victims may project their self-disappointment onto others, making them overly judgmental of situations and persons. This behavior tends to drive others away, thus creating further isolation. In addition, other signs of depression may appear: changes in sleeping and eating patterns, constant irritability, lack of enthusiasm or energy.

The impact on collaboration is blatantly evident. Who would be attracted to minister with someone whose actions offer such repelling messages? In essence, they are proclaiming, "Come collaborate with me and you will be just like me: boring, sad, tired, and depressed!" Is it surprising that people suffering from burnout repel rather than attract people to minister with them?

Stage Four—Terminal Cynicism

The fourth stage of burnout is characterized by terminal cynicism. Persons at this stage experience an erosion of self-esteem. Frequently the lowered self-esteem is manifested as free-floating hostility; friends, co-workers, and everyone around are treated as adversaries and are subject to constant condemnation. Persons in these last two stages often cannot accept support and encouragement from friends and will need the assistance of a professional therapist.

The concept of terminal cynicism is almost visual. The terminal cynic is the one who becomes a "knocker" of everyone and everything. This person experiences a sense of self-loathing and projects it onto anyone with whom they come into contact.

Recommendations for Dealing With Burnout

Individuals experiencing burnout are usually incapable of reversing the downward spiral by themselves. They need peers who love them enough to confront them. You can help these individuals by confronting them about their self-destructive behavior. Realize that when a person in the process of burnout is confronted, the most normal response will be hostility.

Burnout results from a set of potentially debilitating beliefs and attitudes. The primary antidote for burnout is to explore those beliefs that affect behavior and to seek help in changing those beliefs that are self-destructive. If the description of burnout bears some resemblance to the person you have become, we recommend:

1. Give someone in your life the responsibility and the authority to challenge you when you begin to internalize and behave out of unrealistic expectations.
2. Allow others to use their gifts to minister to you. It is often more comfortable to minister to others than allow other to minister to you.
3. Be as kind, gentle, loving, compassionate, and forgiving toward yourself as you are to those to whom you minister.
4. Finally, follow the model of Jesus in the gospels. Learn to say, "no" and to set limits.

Table 4.2

Summary of Stages of Burnout

Stages	Indicators	Behaviors
I. Obsessive, exclusive commitment to ministry	belief system that links work with personal worth	one-dimensional person, no interests outside of ministry, limited support systems, inability to set limits
II. Exhaustion and questioning	physical and psychological exhaustion combined with intense questioning of personal worth	constant tiredness, lack of enthusiasm, uncertainty about life's direction, personal worth, and the value of ministry

	Stages	Indicators	Behaviors
Table 4.2 (continued)	III. Withdrawal and disappointment	withdrawal, disappointment with self and ministry, depression	avoidance of others, judgmental attitude, emotional and physical isolation, depression
	IV. Terminal cynicism	cynicism, low self-esteem	free-floating hostility, "turned off" to everything, constantly condemning, energy focused on survival

While burnout is an obstacle, we also believe that the opposite, "rustout," is equally deleterious. Among full-time ministers today, there are some who have become so consumed with catering to their own needs that they have lost the zeal which is essential for mission.

Hostility

Before discussing hostility as an obstacle, it is important to make a distinction between anger and hostility. Anger, like any emotion, is neither good nor bad, neither positive nor negative (CCC, #1772, 1776). Feeling angry is not sinful, nor does it necessarily interfere with collaboration. Anger is simply a spontaneous reaction to some stimulus. Usually anger can be traced to one of three causes: frustration, a blow to self-esteem, or a perceived injustice. When one or more of these causes is experienced, a person feels angry. Anger, like all emotions, produces energy. This energy can be used to overcome the frustration, to build up the self-esteem, or to overcome the injustice. In other words, it can be used constructively and creatively to build collaboration.

Where then is the problem? The problem lies in the fact that often feelings of anger are converted into hostility. While anger is an emotion, hostility moves beyond an emotion to become a behavior. one that often leads to treating others as enemies. The presence of hostility poses one of the barriers to developing collaboration. Where hostility exists, others are perceived as adversaries to be overcome, rather than as potential allies.

Unfortunately, acknowledging anger is unacceptable for many people, especially ministers. A study of priests in the United States identified the inability to be in touch with and accept their feelings and needs as one of the major problems of the clergy and others in ministry. When left unrecognized or denied, anger is converted into hostility. On a positive note, we have observed a decrease in the degree of hostility among ministers from then to now. This is largely due to efforts at increased dialogue and understanding at many different levels in the church.

One thing is certain: anyone in ministry will experience frustration, blows to self-esteem and injustices. Feelings of anger are inevitable. The challenge is to discover constructive avenues of expressing anger rather than converting it into hostility which ultimately destroys any collaborative efforts taking place.

Failure to Deal With Conflict

The Acts of the Apostles describes the early church as being of one mind and heart and sharing all things in common (4:32). But this description gives only one dimension of the early church. In other sections of the scriptures another dimension emerges. Numerous incidents of dissension and disagreement are recounted: the disciples argue over who is most important (Mk 9:3-34), Paul and certain members of the church of Jerusalem come into conflict over the Gentile question (Acts 15), Paul and Barnabas fight over whether to take Mark with them on their journey (Acts 15:36-39), Paul opposes Peter in public (Gal 2:11-14), and many other examples besides.

Looking at the total picture we see a divinely founded church whose members are very human and where conflict is inevitable. *The Notre Dame Study on Catholic Parish Life* states that the absence of conflict is more likely a sign of rigor mortis than of vitality and community. Suppressing conflict in any group results in apathy and tension which preclude collaboration. If collaboration is to occur, conflict must be confronted and dealt with. Too many ministers are so fearful of conflict that they constantly function from a stance of "peace at any price," not realizing that the price is really a steep one. Failure to deal with conflict condemns people to a state of non-collaboration.

For now, we are simply indicating that both attitude and lack of skill can interfere with the goal of collaboration. In Chapter 8 we will discuss the skills needed to deal more effectively with conflict.

Lack of Forgiveness

A Christian community is not characterized by the absence of anger, conflict, or hostility, but rather by the presence of forgiveness and attempts at reconciliation. *From Words to Deeds* states: "In some cases, healing and reconciliation may be needed before collaboration can take place."

For now we simply note lack of forgiveness and reconciliation as an obstacle. This issue will be discussed at more length in Chapter 6 (spirituality) and Chapter 8 (conflict).

Failure to Deal With Loss

The impact loss and separation has on both individuals and groups has been viewed differently in recent years. Previously, when a person experienced loss or separation, the common advice given was "to spiritualize the experience." Increased awareness that this approach might be harmful to individual development has led to a stress on integrating these experiences in a more conscious way.

Loss and separation are as inevitable in the Christian community as conflict. The pain and hurt, if unrecognized, can also have detrimental effects on ministry. Experiences of loss are some of the greatest causes of stress in life. Too much stress interferes with people's freedom to be with and for others. Again, as was true for anger, it is not the loss itself that is the problem; the problem is the unwillingness to deal with it.

Any loss is experienced on two levels, *real* and *symbolic*. The feelings caused by loss or separation are not only painful in themselves, but also trigger memories and feelings of previous experiences of deep loss. Since the psyche seems incapable of ever completely dealing with the trauma and grieving involved in the most significant personal losses, it stores part of that unfinished pain. A loss in the present acts as a catalyst to release the unfinished business from the past. This means that people are usually dealing with the feelings of many losses at once, one consciously and many more unconsciously. Understanding this helps to explain why seemingly insignificant losses can often arouse such strong emotions.

Many conflicts that arise can also be attributed to feelings of loss. The behavior of a parish council, for example, that spends endless hours in heated discussion over such issues as the removal of church statues or the replacement of traditional hymnals can be explained by understanding the symbolic nature of loss. In some cases the current issue serves as a symbol for more significant losses such as the relocation of a favorite staff member or even the pervasive loss of the familiar church they knew before the Second Vatican Council. The more that a person's sense of identity is intrinsically linked with a particular group, organization, or parish, the more intense will be the feelings of loss if the continued existence of that group as he or she knows it is threatened.

When feelings of loss are denied or not dealt with, they interfere with the ability to minister collaboratively. Denying the feelings engendered by loss can produce an individual who avoids intimacy and maintains an aloofness from others. Compassion, which is the heart of ministry, cannot be expressed at a distance nor can collaboration occur in isolation.

Realizing that many people in ministry generally experience a high rate of mobility, it should be apparent that greater attention needs to be paid to the experience of loss both for the one leaving and for the ones left behind. Unless the feelings of loss are acknowledged and dealt with, the ability to re-invest in new relationships or situations will be greatly impeded. You can't say hello until you've learned to say goodbye.

Learning to deal with loss can assist in developing more collaborative relationships and ministries. These general suggestions for dealing with loss may prove helpful:

1. Allow yourself to get in touch with and accept your feelings.
2. Speak with others about your feelings (keeping in mind that others may discourage you from discussing your feelings because such discussions may stir up their own unfinished business with losses they have experienced).
3. Find a way to meaningfully ritualize the loss.
4. Allow yourself adequate time to grieve.
5. Permit the death/resurrection theology to become active in your life (e.g., allow new relationships and new life to replace what has been lost).

Lack of Knowledge of Gifts

The essence of collaborative ministry is the identification, release, and union of all the gifts in ministry for the sake of mission. Logically, then, any group wishing to initiate a collaborative project would begin with a discernment of gifts. Too often we encounter groups who have embarked on the path to collaboration without having engaged in a gift discernment process. Suffice it to say here, that failure to identify gifts makes it impossible to collaborate.

Failure to Share Faith

For us, it is inconceivable to expect collaborative ministry to occur when the individuals working together do not share faith. Nevertheless, from our experience, sharing faith seems to be more the exception than the rule among many people in ministry. By sharing faith, we mean more than saying prayers together. We are referring to sharing those graced moments of experiencing God in a special way. For instance, relating the times when people have found God in each other or among the people with whom they are working, or those experiences when one is most aware of God's presence.

People have many reasons for their hesitancy to share faith. For many, their religious training did not foster this style of prayer, and an introduction of prayer that is both communal and personal, rather than private, will probably be met with fear, resistance, or both. For others, shared prayer is scrupulously avoided because it demands a level of trust and intimacy that is too threatening.

The one thing that differentiates a ministry group from any other group is its common mission, the promoting of the reign of God. If the group is to work collaboratively to accomplish that mission, then the members need to pray together and share faith in order to discover how God is calling them communally. We have discovered that groups share faith easily when two conditions are present: (1) a climate that assures safety in sharing, and (2) an expectation that sharing will in fact take place. Not everyone will have the same degree of comfort in this endeavor. Sensitivity and patience are necessary to develop the climate for faith sharing to occur. Chapter 6 contains further discussion of shared spirituality as one element of collaborative spirituality.

Ministry is the expression in action of one's spirituality. It is one's relationship with God overflowing into an action called ministry. Therefore, collaborative ministry is an expression of the group's spirituality into a corporate action.

Lack of an Integrated Sexuality

Ministering in today's church brings people together in personal and intimate ways. This can be threatening for individuals who have difficulty recognizing or appreciating their sexuality. Inadequate sexual integration can prevent participation in and even be counterproductive to collaboration.

Sexuality is a gift; it should be acknowledged, appreciated, and accepted as part of the total person. However, past attitudes toward sexuality led many people in ministry to repress or suppress this aspect of their being. The challenge is to discover ways of expressing sexuality in an integrated way that allows the freedom to enter more fully into ministry with others.

Two indications of a lack of sexual integration are fear and obsession. Some people become inordinately fearful of working with anyone toward whom they might have a sexual attraction. These people often spend an excessive amount of energy suppressing or repressing the normal feelings, thoughts and desires that emerge in the course of daily life— energy that could be channeled into ministerial activities. Beliefs and fears about sexuality render them incapable of the ordinary encounters, relationships, and honest self-revealing dialogue with those with whom they minister, prerequisites for people working together in ministry.

Lack of sexual integration can also give rise to an obsession with the sexual feelings that may emerge during the course of building pastoral or ministerial relationships. As a result, energy becomes obsessively focused on self or on the relationship to the exclusion of ministry. Either of these extreme tendencies is destructive to collaboration.

The last few years have witnessed an increasing interest in the topic of sexuality among ministers. Perhaps this is directly related to the efforts being made toward more collaborative forms of ministry. As people work closely with others on a day-to-day basis, they may be forced to deal more directly with their sexual feelings. As collaborative ministry becomes more commonplace, the need for assistance and education in this area of personal growth will probably become even more apparent.

Psychoanalyst Harold Searles states that people working closely with others in a very personal, intense, helping relationship often discover themselves feeling sexually attracted toward or falling in love with their clients. Citing a number of reasons for this behavior, he suggests that the sexual attraction or the falling in love is not the problem; what is potentially problematic is the denial of this reality. All feelings are communicated, even unconscious ones. People working in close collaborative relationships should not be surprised to feel strong emotional attractions. If these feelings are not acknowledged and accepted and, when appropriate, even discussed together or with a third party, difficulties in ministry will ensue.

Given the fact that personal histories may make it difficult for some ministers to accept sexual attractions and feelings, we strongly recommend ongoing consultation and supervision for all people in ministry. This supervision/consultation helps in uncovering and working through some of the unconscious elements that interfere with the ability to be an effective minister.

We also recommend that those involved in collaborative ministry attend sexuality workshops to aid in the greater integration of this profound aspect of life. The best sexuality workshops for people in ministry are conducted by those who are comfortable with their own sexuality, have a thorough knowledge of the field, and possess a deep understanding and respect for the Christian attitudes toward sexuality. In conducting sexuality workshops, we have been impressed with the intense need and willingness on the part of so many ministers—women, men, lay, clergy and religious—to discuss this aspect of their lives honestly and openly.

Learned Helplessness

Although the term "learned helplessness," as used by Leonore Walker, author of *The Battered Woman*, is normally used to describe an attitude held by victims of physical abuse, the concept may be applied to an undesirable form of behavior that often stands in the way of moving toward greater collaboration.

Learned helplessness is an attitude toward life that constantly results in a feeling of being victimized. In studying the victims of physical abuse, researchers have discovered that these people believe that as a result of past experiences, they have no control over their lives. They are firmly convinced that no matter what they do, it will not effect change; therefore, they develop a general attitude of passivity and hopelessness. The attitude becomes so ingrained that even when a successful outcome is realized, they tend to dismiss the reality and continue believing that they are helpless. The reality is not as important as the perception of the reality, and the perception leads to passive, submissive behavior.

The theory has profound implications for people in ministry. Frequently we encounter people who have developed a basic attitude of learned helplessness, believing they have absolutely no control over any decisions regarding their lives and ministry. They believe that someone outside themselves, usually someone in authority, has all the power, and that it would be useless for them to attempt to change even a difficult or a destructive situation. They feel victimized and angry. However, they are usually the same people for whom anger is an unacceptable emotion, so they store it in a way that leads to physical illness, depression, or passive-aggressive behavior.

People who function from a stance of learned helplessness have often grown up or been formed in a system in which they have been the recipients of continual negative reinforcement. They enter adulthood with low self-image, minimum self-confidence, and diminished self-esteem. They have difficulty accepting and appreciating their own personal resources and gifts. As a result, collaboration is very difficult for them. Their attitude of absolute helplessness and hopelessness seriously impedes their ability to take initiative, and they do not see the value in working with others to try to better a situation. Their attitude has a paralyzing effect on them.

There are instances where individuals and groups are overcoming this tendency to learned helplessness. In one parish, for example, the parishioners were informed of the imminent transfer of their pastor. Instead of passively awaiting a new pastor, they requested a meeting with the bishop in order to indicate the type of pastor they believed would be best for the parish.

People who adopt a posture of learned helplessness need the assistance of others to help them take initiative and reassess their capacity to bring about change. Since learned helplessness is the result of negative reinforcement, it takes a great deal of positive reinforcement and support to bring about the desired change.

Conclusion

The more an individual faces his or her shadow side, personal demons, or obstacles to collaboration, the more committed one will become. Most individuals find it difficult to engage in the process of naming one's own inadequacies. The human psyche expends much energy in avoiding this onerous task. Difficult though it may be, surfacing obstacles is the single most important factor in facilitating collaborative ministry. Once these demons have been identified it takes hard work to exorcise them since they have often become part of our way of acting.

Reflection/Discussion Questions

1. Besides the obstacles listed here, what are additional obstacles to collaboration that I see in myself? How do I intend to overcome these obstacles?
2. Can I identify at least one obstacle to my becoming more committed to collaborative ministry? How do I plan to work on this obstacle?
3. Which of the obstacles listed in this chapter trigger an emotional response in me? What areas do I need to investigate further?

5

Readiness for Collaborative Ministry

Collaboration occurs as the result of a deliberate choice. This choice can be made effectively only by those who show a developmental readiness for collaboration. Specifically, the more fully developed a person is psycho-sexually, the greater is the person's capacity to minister collaboratively. When people achieve the level of development called *generativity*, they experience more fullness of life and are capable of collaboration.

One of the main reasons why there may be such a gap between the desire for collaboration and its actuality is that quite a few of those attempting to collaborate do not have the capacity or capability: they do not possess the maturity to collaborate. We hope that acknowledging that reality does not provide a rationale for avoiding collaboration on the part of those looking for reasons to avoid it. Rather, we hope that the reality serves as a challenge to everyone involved in collaboration to earnestly focus their attention on their psycho-sexual development.

Everyone possesses the potential to become a complete, mature individual, the "generative person" defined by Erik Erikson. God creates people with an innate orientation toward growth and, given normal conditions, individuals move in that direction. In Erikson's model the goal of normal human development is twofold: to become generative and to develop a sense of integrity. To become generative means to grow in the ability to care for others; to develop a sense of integrity means being at peace in the knowledge of one's self, one's accomplishments, and one's limitations. When people act with generativity and integrity, ministry results.

A generative adult ministers as a self-giving, other-centered person and can function either independently or with others. The generative person trusts others enough to co-minister in gospel-oriented projects. He or she is willing to initiate new projects, risk new ideas, or support the creative ventures of others even when criticism may be encountered. Generative people are comfortable with their own human limits and frailty. They are, in Henri Nouwen's words, "wounded healers" who can allow others to see their woundedness and sinfulness because they believe they will be loved in spite of their limitations.

Those who attempt to function at the generative level before they have successfully completed the earlier stages lack spontaneity, joy, and excitement in what they are doing. Their ministry is burdensome. They are not usually motivated by being and doing for others; rather, their ministry is almost exclusively self-fulfilling. These ministers are especially prone to burnout.

Individuals grow to the generative level of development when two elements are present: challenge and models. As Christians we need to challenge each other to grow. And we must allow others to challenge us. Models are also important. Those individuals whose lives reflect a continual pattern of growth, despite their own human shortcomings and struggles, can help others set realistic life goals. Unfortunately, the models offered to ministers have sometimes been so perfectionistic that attempting to imitate them is more likely to be frustrating than helpful.

We interviewed forty-two Christians in the marketplace who are effective ministers in their work arena. Their lives, as reported in *The Collaborative Leader*, are characterized as people of integrity, filled with life, and generative. When asked to identify the values which motivated them, they consistently repeated the same qualities. First, they are people for whom compassion is a major motivating force. Compassion was the most frequently mentioned word used in describing themselves. The criteria for assessing generativity is the presence of an ever-expanding compassion that reaches out to touch others in ever-widening circles.

The second quality of these people whom we dubbed "wisdom people" is that they are compelled to "do the right thing" regardless of the consequences or personal cost to themselves. This stance toward life is what characterizes a person of integrity. It should come as no surprise that these wisdom people also place great emphasis on working as a team, working collaboratively. Because of their level of psycho-sexual development, they have the capacity to be collaborative and can minister collaboratively.

Introduction to Erikson's Model for Psycho-Sexual Development

Erikson's model (Table 5.1) is based upon the belief that people develop sequentially through stages as they mature, with each stage building on the previous ones.

Table 5.1	*Erikson's Epigenetic Model of Psycho-Sexual Development* 1. Trust vs. Mistrust 2. Autonomy vs. Shame or Doubt 3. Initiative vs. Guilt 4. Industry vs. Inferiority 5. Identity vs. Identity Diffusion 6. Intimacy vs. Isolation 7. Generativity vs. Stagnation 8. Integrity vs. Despair

Only after successfully completing the tasks of the earlier stages can the person reach the stages of generativity and integrity. Failure to adequately resolve the tasks of any particular stage interferes with normal development. The issues of that stage arise again in later life.

This chapter addresses a model for evaluating psycho-sexual development and, therefore, readiness for collaboration. As human beings we are not finished products; we are always in the process of becoming. Therefore, we begin with the presupposition that there are some aspects in each of us that are less than fully developed. This is not a negative assessment but rather an invitation to further growth.

We urge readers to focus on self-evaluation rather than using this model to assess and judge others with whom they are engaged in ministry. Our goal is to help each reader evaluate his or her readiness and capacity for collaboration. We describe some behaviors that characterize development at the stages preceding generativity and integrity. We challenge each reader to seek a friend, counselor, or spiritual director who can assist in this assessment. Often, when the assessment is done in isolation, without the honest feedback of others, self-delusion can occur.

Trust

Collaboration is based on the ability to relate to others. All relationships presuppose the capacity to trust. Trust requires an underlying belief that the other person is basically "for" you and does not intend harm. When the earliest experiences in life reinforce this belief, an individual develops a capacity for trust. A trusting person has:

— the ability to differentiate between those who can be trusted and those individuals, based on past experience, who cannot be trusted;
— a basic attitude that others intend good, not harm;
— the ability to enter relationships anticipating acceptance and trustworthiness rather than rejection.

Trust, as is true for all of the developmental stages, is not something achieved once and forever. When there has been a breach of trust, there is a need to renegotiate one's decision to trust. Sometimes, in the process of collaboration there is a breakdown of trust. Something occurs which changes the attitude from believing that others intend good to a belief based on an experience that others intend harm. Sadly, there are individuals, who because there has been a breach of trust, have simply withdrawn and refused to take any initiative to re-establish trust. Each one bears individual responsibility for attempting to reinstate a climate and attitude of trust. Collaboration is impossible unless there is a basic trust among the individuals involved.

Autonomy

A small child is completely dependent upon adults. As the child begins to experience a sense of self, he or she feels a need to express this new-found autonomy. The classic example is the small child who learns and almost obsessively repeats the word "no."

Collaboration requires the ability to function both independently and cooperatively. Certain people in ministry have been rewarded for being dependent and submissive, and sometimes have experienced subtle punishment for acting autonomously. This makes it difficult for them to grow to this stage and collaborate with others.

Autonomous adults are able to:

— be self-governing;
— avoid being overly self-reliant or independent;
— listen to suggestions from others, especially those in authority, without automatically reacting negatively or defensively;
— appreciate their uniqueness;
— make decisions contrary to the rules, even when there is the possibility of rejection;
— enjoy a sense of control in their lives because they are willing to make choices, even difficult ones.

There are some people who seem to lack individuality and who appear to be merely an extension of another. They have no independent thoughts or opinions. They think and speak through others. There is a symbiotic attachment between these individuals that precludes their ability to make personal decisions. They are fixated at the level of autonomy and do not have the capacity to collaborate.

Initiative

At this third stage the child develops the capacity to take initiative and begins to assume personal responsibility for choices. At times, collaboration demands taking risks and attempting new things, in spite of possible failure. Ministers who have developed initiative are able to minister creatively and are willing to try new models of ministry.

People who have developed initiative:

— accept life's setbacks without failure-producing paralysis;
— are able to begin and maintain projects;
— make innovative decisions about life and ministry;
— identify personal goals and live by them;
— take the initiative in changing difficult, painful situations;
— do not allow fear of criticism or condemnation (from themselves or from others) to prevent them from taking action.

Those who have not developed a capacity for initiative are fearful of engaging in activity which could end in failure. They have almost an obsession with success. Those who collaborate will fail often. The potential of failure is always present when trying something new and different. A 1999 article in the International Herald Tribune compared the moribund atmosphere of Washington, DC with the energy of the Silicon Valley. The author, David Ignatius, concluded that the companies in the Silicon Valley, "would not be growing so fast if they were not making mistakes along the way and learning from them." In other words, those companies are willing to take initiative, even if it results in failure. By comparison, Washington, D.C., is described as "a compulsive, risk-averse, excuse-making, blame-shifting, afraid-of-falling-off-the-greasy-pole kind of town." Washington, the author writes, is "driven by an ingrained intolerance of failure."

How does this comparison describe what is experienced in church? Are leaders encouraged to tolerate failure or are climates created that eschew any attempts that could end in failure? Do they encourage a spirituality of failure?

Industry

By *industry* Erikson means the capacity to work cooperatively with others. This stage occurs developmentally when a child moves away from the exclusiveness of the home and plays with other children. Ideally the child becomes less self-centered and learns to "give and take." Even the child's vocabulary reflects this change, moving from an exclusive use of "I" to "we."

Collaboration ideally goes far beyond mere working together, but it is only when people reach this stage that there are the beginnings of collaboration.

Those with a capacity for industry

— work cooperatively at task-oriented activities;
— recognize the value of working cooperatively;
— enter into situations that require "give and take";
— identify and value specific areas of personal competence and achievement and have acquired some level of self-esteem;
— are free from over-competitiveness;
— are oriented toward the success of the group;
— are able to share on the level of ideas.

While those who have developed their capacity for industry can work together, they have achieved only the minimum ability to collaborate. Collaboration involves more than merely engaging in cooperative tasks with others. It involves the ability to relate in a personal way and to share faith and intimacy in addition to performing tasks.

Identity

Forming *self-identity* is the developmental stage of the adolescent, the person in transition from childhood to adulthood. The primary task of this stage is to grapple with the sense of one's own identity. It is a movement back from the "we" to a new understanding of "I." Adolescence is a time of self-confrontation, of assessing personal strengths and weaknesses. There may be reluctance to accept fully this newly-discovered self. New emotions, physical changes, and the realization of limitations and inadequacies create high anxiety, a characteristic of persons at this stage. This is one of the stages that comes to the forefront at mid-life. Here individuals again grapple, though at a deeper level, with an sense of identity that no longer has the idealism of youth.

People who have successfully accomplished the tasks of this stage accept themselves as unique individuals with limited gifts and strengths. They can engage in projects without expending undue energy in preventing others from knowing the "real me." They do not fear that they will lose their self-identity in collaborating.

Ministers with a strong self-identity

— are aware of their positive and negative attributes and are comfortable with themselves;
— have realistic expectations of themselves and others;
— relate freely with others as equals;
— become comfortable with their sexuality;
— relate well with those in authority;
— make choices, even when others disapprove;
— are able to make work commitments;
— are not unduly influenced by heroes, idols, organizations, or communities;
— are more flexible in thinking and decision-making.

If those who achieve the stage of industry are at the basic or first level of collaboration, those who develop a sense of identity are at a second level of collaboration. They are coming to an awareness of their personal giftedness and realize that they can bring these gifts to collaborative efforts. However, they still lack the ability to relate at an intimate level with those with whom they find themselves with in mutual collaboration.

Intimacy

In this stage of development the young adult is ready to risk sharing his or her newly discovered sense of identity with another. Secure in some knowledge of self, a person is free to merge with others without fear of losing his or her identity in the process. How individuals resolve the tension between intimacy and isolation will have an impact on their effectiveness in ministry.

When an adequate degree of intimacy is not reached, people are limited simply to performing the task at hand. Resolving the tasks of this stage, however, brings the ability to form commitments, to live communally, and to minister mutually. Intimacy allows people to move beyond simply performing tasks with others: it enables them to share themselves and their faith.

Those who have developed their capacity for intimacy are able to

— establish, build, and maintain relationships (more than one);
— share on many levels, for example: work, faith, experiences, feelings;
— share their positive and negative aspects with others;
— relate comfortably to both sexes;
— feel love deeply and love deeply in return.

As is evident, those who develop their capacity for intimacy can bring their whole being to the process of collaboration. They are generative in the way described at the start of this chapter. Not only do they desire to work collaboratively, but they possess the ability to do so.

Table 5.2 provides a simple review of the stages preceding generativity and integrity. Only those who have successfully mastered the stages from trust to intimacy have the potential to act generatively and as people of integrity.

Table 5.2 *From Trust to Intimacy*

Stage	Developed	Undeveloped	Negative Impact on Collaboration
I.Trust- believes that others are favorably inclined	basic trust, but selective mistrust	trusts no one, trusts indiscrim- inately	unable to work with others; needs solitary projects

	Stage	Developed	Undeveloped	Negative Impact on Collaboration
Table 5.2 *(continued)*	II. *Autonomy-* is able to function as a separate person	independent; self-governing	conforming or compliant; excessively dependent or completely independent; obstinate, controlling, manipulative	clings to co-workers; needs to control any project
	III. *Initiative-* takes personal responsibility	begins and maintains projects; self-starter	fears failure (does nothing); never checks with authority	can only engage in activities that pose no risk of failure
	IV. *Industry-* works and plays cooperatively	task-oriented; cooperative	obsessive idividualism	cannot be part of a project with others
	V. *Identity-* has a sense of self	self-assured; accurate self-perception; comfortable with self	fears loss of self; over-identifies with group; defensive, arrogant	not aware of what they bring to the collaborative effort; doesn't know limits
	VI. *Intimacy-* has the capacity to share self	shares life, ministry, prayer; close friendships	cold, reserved; fears sharing	stays on the periphery of groups; never engages with others

Conclusion

Not everyone who wants to collaborate has the ability to do so. Some lack the capacity because they have not yet matured to the point where they are psycho-sexually capable of collaborating. This should not be perceived as a source of hopelessness. Erik Erikson points out in his later works that individuals rework the developmental stages throughout their lives. In so doing, there is the opportunity to renegotiate some of the earlier life tasks that were less than developed. Every person possesses the capacity for growth if one is willing to address the various issues and tasks of growth in a concerted way. As mentioned earlier, everyone needs people in their lives who can help assess the level of development and assist in the slow process of maturing.

Reflection/Discussion Questions

1. At what level of psycho-sexual development am I? How do I know this? Am I willing to discuss this with objective others who will give me honest feedback?
2. What are the next steps that I must take in my growth toward greater maturity? How will I evaluate this growth?
3. What are some of the areas I may need to further strengthen:
   - Do I trust others?
   - Can I function independently of others?
   - Am I able to take responsibility for my self and my actions?
   - Can I work with others?
   - Am I comfortable with the person I am?
   - Am I able to form relationships with others?

6

Spirituality for Collaborative Ministry

Ministry is the embodiment and expression of spirituality. While an action may be good, it is not ministry unless it is an expression and an overflow of one's relationship with God. By baptism all Christians are called to holiness and to ministry, that is, to a spirituality which has two dimensions, a deepened relationship with God and an expression of that relationship in action.

Spirituality for any ministry, including collaborative ministry, is first and foremost an active spirituality. This statement has been validated by many church leaders and scholars. Pope John Paul II emphasized this concept of an active spirituality: "Christianity is . . . a religion of God's action and of man (and woman's) action" (CTH, p. 128).

The USCCB has likewise emphasized an active spirituality that embraces all of life, and at its core is an Incarnational spirituality. The bishops presented a question—"What does it mean to be a holy or spiritual person?"—and then offered this answer:

> To be holy is to live according to the gospel . . . It is the ever present challenge to be a people of heartfelt compassion, kindness, humility, gentleness, patience, and forgiveness (Cf: Col 3:12). It is a call to embrace the beatitudes (Mt 5:3-11) . . . It is an invitation to bring a heightened sense of the presence of Jesus Christ into the regular rhythms of life: going to school or work, raising a family, and participating in civic life (SDL, p. 18).

Theologian Kenneth Himes claims that as a result of the Second Vatican Council document *Gaudium et spes*,

> [s]pirituality could no longer be seen as a retreat from the world but an invitation to enter into the depth dimension of worldly life (WTC).

And, commenting on research done by the Jesuit sociologist, John Coleman, Himes concludes that,

> American Catholicism is not experiencing a spiritual crisis but in fact a spiritual renaissance. . . . We are experiencing . . . a structural crisis. . . . The real problem is finding ways whereby people can act upon the spirituality and the vitality and the faith that they have (WTC).

Since writing our first book on collaborative ministry we have spent countless hours listening to women and men in all states of life talk about their spirituality. Some more insights about spirituality have come from these encounters. (Six of these insights are listed in Table 6.1.)

Table 6.1   *Insights About Spirituality*

1. There is not just one systematically formed model of spirituality for ministry.
2. There are some clearly discernable elements of a spirituality for collaborative ministry.
3. People hunger for a spirituality, a deep personal relationship with God.
4. Spirituality is primarily one's relationship with God as it affects every aspect of a person's life.
5. Spirituality is relational and affects one's relationship with others and with the environment.
6. Two core elements of a life-giving spirituality for collaborative ministers are compassion and forgiveness.

Many individuals have formulated beliefs about spirituality which are often narrow and constricting. Their beliefs frequently restrict the ways in which the Holy Spirit is revealed.

As an example, too many ministers, especially lay men and lay women and contemporary men and women religious, measure their spirituality against the spirituality lived by past generations of men and women religious. The monastic, often individualistic spirituality of the past suited the lifestyles of religious communities of the time. However, these forms of spirituality may not meet the needs of people ministering today in collaborative styles.

For example, congregations who have revised their constitutions and documents since the Second Vatican Council often articulate challenging, prophetic mission statements, yet make few changes in the sections on spirituality from former documents. This can prove extremely stressful and guilt-producing for those members who attempt to be responsive to the newly-defined mission and ministry demands while at the same time striving to be faithful to the spiritual practices and devotions of a different period.

In addition, popular writers on spirituality, who offer a great service to the church, seem to find it difficult to distance themselves from religious-congregation-based value systems regarding spirituality and to articulate a radically different spirituality for today's collaborative ministers.

In no way do we intend to minimize the spirituality of the past which has nurtured and enriched so many lives. We simply offer some observations and reflections based on what we have learned from our listening sessions. The elements of a spirituality for collaborative ministry that have surfaced most frequently from these sessions are listed in Table 6.2 and summarized in the text that follows.

Table 6.2	*Elements of a Spirituality for Collaborative Ministry*
	1. It moves to compassionate action.
	2. It encompasses forgiveness.
	3. It is reflective.
	4. It is shared.
	5. It fits the person.
	6. It is affective.
	7. It is able to integrate failure.

A Spirituality Which Moves to Compassionate Action

This element of a life-giving spirituality has two aspects: compassion and forgiveness. Compassion is the ultimate criteria for determining one's growth in the spiritual life. St. Theresa of Avila counseled that there is only one true crucible for testing prayer, and that is compassion. An USCCB document enfleshes the concept of compassion, describing the forms it takes in daily life:

> The journey toward holiness is the path towards finding and satisfying our hunger for meaning, making something worthwhile out of our lives. It urges us to reach beyond ourselves in service to our families and other relationships, to our work, to our communities and to our Church, to be zealous in the pursuit of justice for the poor, the marginalized, the unborn, the elderly, the suffering, and the brokenhearted (SDL, p. 18f).

Jesus is the exemplar of compassion. Throughout the gospels we see his compassionate response to everyone in need. It is Jesus who provides a challenge to all his followers when he commands: "Be compassionate as your Father is compassionate" (Lk 6:36). For a spirituality to be truly Christlike, it must be characterized by compassionate action.

James Fenhagen, author of *Invitation to Holiness*, describes compassion as "love empowered by holiness." The *Webster's Third New International Dictionary* defines compassion as "a spiritual consciousness of personal tragedy of another and selfless tenderness directed toward it." Compassion requires the ability to move beyond feeling and thinking to action. Note that the dictionary refers to compassion as a "spiritual consciousness." It flows from the depths of one's relationship with God.

In *Compassion: A Reflection on the Christian Life*, Donald McNeill, Douglas Morrison, and Henri Nouwen indicate why this particular act of the will is difficult:

> It is important . . . to recognize that suffering is not something we desire or to which we are attracted. On the contrary, it is something we want to avoid at all costs. Therefore, compassion is not among our natural responses.

Compassion not only conveys an understanding of another's pain or suffering, but reaches out to alleviate that suffering. This type of response stems from an experience of God's love and from a decision to express that love in action. It is through compassionate action that ministry becomes the embodiment of spirituality. Compassion is the linchpin where ministry and spirituality converge.

Careful attention reveals that the word compassion frequently occurs in conversation. Perhaps due in part to a highly technological, depersonalized society, compassion is emerging as a need in today's world. A need is something so vital that unless it is met to some degree a person becomes sick or dies emotionally, spiritually, and sometimes physically. The world contains many people who are emotionally, spiritually, or physically sick and dying because they do not experience compassion from others. Scores of people experience great loneliness and need a compassionate response from members of the Christian community. Since ministry is the intentional response to a need, then a true spirituality expresses itself in compassionate responses to those in need.

"When have you felt ministered to?" is a question we frequently pose in parishes. The most common response is that a person feels ministered to when there has been a compassionate response. One man shared his experience after the death of a child. While many friends offered advice, it was those whose physical presence and verbal consolation expressed compassion who helped him the most. Their response conveyed to him their actual presence with him in suffering. McNeill et al. describe this as true compassion:

> What really counts is that in moments of pain and suffering someone stays with us. More important than any particular action or word of advice is the simple presence of someone who cares.

Truly Christ-like compassion is not selective but universal in its expression. Jesus reaches out to everyone. Our response as Christians cannot be limited but should extend to anyone we encounter. A *Hindustan Times Sunday Magazine* article presented words from beggars, outcasts in Indian society, asking them if they recalled any acts of human kindness. One beggar responded:

> In my eight years of begging, I can recall only one instance of real compassion. I was ill and sitting on a patri [a low wooden stool] outside the town hall. I hadn't eaten for several days. I sat crouched up in my durry [carpet], sobs of grief racking my body. A sardar [sikh] walked past me. He stopped and came back. He didn't say anything. He just led me to a tea shop, bought me some buns and tea. We sat together silently. Then he walked away into the night.

Upon hearing this story of the beggar, a woman at one of our presentations related her own story. During the Great Depression, her parents died and she was invited to live with an aunt. The aunt provided her with a place to sleep on the floor, but there was no food to share. One day she left the house in search of a job. She was so weak she could barely walk. A stranger, noticing her, invited her into a diner. He bought her tea, soup, and toast. He then gave her a dime so she could take the subway to a place where she obtained a job.

Clearly these modern versions of the Good Samaritan parable provide a lesson in compassion. Each day presents the challenge to discover those who need compassion—in the home, in the rectory, in the religious house, in the work place, and in the neighborhood.

Who are the "beggars" that you pass each day?

A Spirituality Which Encompasses Forgiveness

The second definitive element of a spirituality for collaborative ministry is forgiveness. Anger, hostility, violence, and conflict appear to be prevalent in current society. These actions exist in the Christian community as well. However, it is not the absence of anger, hostility, or conflict which characterizes the Christian church, but the presence of forgiveness and the attempts at reconciliation.

As we begin the third millennium, the church is calling Christians to witness forgiveness and reconciliation to a world which is in great need of healing and unity. Forgiveness and reconciliation are the only antidotes for brokenness and violence. Pope John Paul II stressed this call to forgiveness in his writings for the new millennium, calling the Jubilee Year 2000 "a year of reconciliation" (CTM). Bishop Pilla declared to the General Meeting of the United States Conference of Catholic Bishops that,

> A spirit of reconciliation is . . . the essence of our being Christ's disciples and our ability to carry out the mission which the Lord gave into our care.

Forgiveness has the potential to transform any human relationship. However, forgiveness is never an easy virtue to acquire. The normal human reaction is to hold on to anger and resentment, and to withhold forgiveness. Yet doing so is self-destructive as well as detrimental to mission. Pope John Paul also wrote:

> We nourish our anger as though it will produce a reparation that continues to accrue, like interest owed on an unpaid debt. The grudge can become a part of us, something too precious to renounce (CTM, p. 3).

The very essence of the Christian life is forgiveness. Forgiveness is an act of the will. It is deciding to let go of the desire to get even with or harm someone who has offended or harmed you. Sometimes individuals can manufacture a myriad of rationalizations for withholding forgiveness. What excuses do you advance for delaying or avoiding forgiveness? The book and movie *Dead Man Walking* is familiar to many people. A subsequent book, *Forgiving the Dead Man Walking*, is not as well-known. The book was written by Deborah Morris, who was raped by Robert Willie, the real-life character played by Sean Penn in the movie. Morris recounts that after fifteen years she has reached a point where she is able to forgive Willie. Forgiveness is a slow process that cannot be rushed. Morris came to the realization that as long as she held on to her anger and did not forgive, she continued to be a victim of Willie. She wrote that,

> The refusal to forgive him always meant that I held onto all my Robert Willie-related stuff—my pain, my shame, my self-pity. That's what I gave up in forgiving him. And it wasn't until I did, that real healing could even begin.

Forgiveness is both an act of immense spirituality and a gift to oneself. Chapter 8 further develops the theme of forgiveness.

A Spirituality Which Is Reflective

Friendship with God, like any human relationship, requires time to deepen and nurture the bond of love. This friendship cannot develop into fullness without a reflective spiritual life. Quiet moments of prayer and reflection allow us to touch the source of life within, to gain knowledge of ourselves as gifted persons, and to ponder God's continuing call and our response. Yet many ministers voice a concern that their overly demanding ministerial lives cause their spiritual lives to suffer as they are able to find little time to be reflective.

True collaboration is impossible unless it flows from one's relationship with God. To nurture such a relationship demands reflective time:

> This means individual and group prayer, time for reflection and faith sharing, and attentive listening to the Spirit in our midst (FWD, p. 21).

Pre-conceived ideas about models of reflection may impose obstacles that need not exist. Bishop Hubbard challenges people to think about a model of reflection in which one does not withdraw from ordinary life, but rather discovers ways to integrate that reflection into the ebb and flow of daily life. In *Fulfilling the Vision: Collaborative Ministry in the Parish*, he wrote:

> In the past . . . the church encouraged or seemed to have encouraged lay people to find holiness by leaving the world instead of finding holiness in the world. Now the laity must take the initiative to recapture and to develop practical ways to implement that sterling insight of the Council that their unique role as laity is to make Christ present in society and to transform political, economic and social institutions in light of the gospel.

The concept of an active spirituality poses a unique challenge for clergy and members of religious congregations.

Priests and religious whose formation was in a quiet atmosphere removed from the hustle and bustle of normal daily life, may experience difficulty learning to be reflective in a hectic ministerial setting. Most laity, on the other hand, have developed their spirituality in milieus similar to the ones in which they find themselves ministering. They have often developed a greater capacity to reflect in the midst of constant activity. Our experience in conducting parish programs confirms this fact. For example, homemakers recount a normal day which starts with being awakened by an infant's cries and ends with collapsing into bed exhausted. These same individuals talk about a deep relationship with God which has been fostered by finding moments in the midst of their daily tasks to converse intimately with God.

In conducting workshops in parishes, we often ask participants where they pray. Common responses are: the bathroom, the bedroom, the automobile, the kitchen, and nature. (One woman told us she had stained glass windows installed in the bathroom.) Unable to seek isolation, these people have developed the skill of reflecting in the midst of hectic situations. They can teach others how to do this.

Some time ago we met with a group in the home of one of its members, a mother with seven children, one of whom had died. Three of the children had muscular dystrophy, which placed great time and energy demands on the parents. During a session in which we utilized a discernment model (described in Chapter 10), the group members told the woman the gifts they saw in her. It became evident that she was a spiritual woman of deep faith who radiated this spirituality, faith, and peace to everyone she encountered. Later, as she spoke about her spirituality, she described using whatever moments she could "steal" in the course of her extremely demanding days to develop her relationship with God. She is a model for her Christian community as she integrates reflection into her pressured life.

Like this mother, we need to function on two levels at the same time—being completely present to what we are doing while learning to "steal moments" to be aware of the presence of God.

A Spirituality Which Is Shared

During a workshop on the topic of shared ministry, a sister commented that if religious are to develop an apostolic spirituality to sustain and nourish them in the midst of a hectic life, they must be willing to learn from the laity who have developed a rich spirituality without the luxury of the prolonged prayer and contemplation times afforded many priests and religious. Clergy and religious, on the other hand, can offer the fruits of a spirituality developed through more structured formation. Priests, religious, and laity will come to a fuller and richer spirituality when they acknowledge their own gifts and the gifts of others. This, however, requires humility. Sometimes arrogance blinds people to seeing and learning from others and prevents further development in the spiritual life.

Collaboration in ministry demands collaboration in spirituality. No one group can assume the stance of "experts" while others remain "learners." There must be a willingness and an openness to listen and to learn from those in different lifestyles. If behavior is a way of evaluating beliefs and values, then one way of evaluating openness is to determine the extent to which we have allowed others, particularly those in different lifestyles, to influence our spirituality.

We saw this openness emerge at a workshop on lay ministries requested by a congregation of men religious and attended by the religious, parishioners, and staff members of parishes. The discussion which followed the presentation on spirituality was highly theoretical and intellectual. The reticence of the lay persons, who had been involved up to this point, was apparent. We asked the lay participants what they were feeling during the discussion. Almost universally they described themselves as "feeling stupid." We then asked the priests and religious present to be silent and to listen. For two and one-half hours the lay people recounted personal stories of faith and prayer which were powerful and deeply moving. One man, a farmer, shared that everyday he would climb on his tractor and begin talking with God. He concluded by saying, "God and I just talk to each other from sunrise to sunset, but of course that's not spirituality, is it?" A woman, who was illiterate, spoke for ten minutes of how she finds God in the land and in her children. In evaluating the workshop, the religious noted this particular session as the most valuable part of the program. These men had benefited immensely by allowing the laity to teach them about spirituality.

Not only must religious and priests be willing to listen to the laity, but they must be willing to share faith experiences with those with whom they minister. Lay men and women comment that they feel deprived because clergy and members of religious congregations rarely share personal stories of their faith with them, including in homilies.

Some religious congregations are developing programs whereby those laity and diocesan clergy who minister in the congregation's apostolates are introduced to the spirituality of the congregation. An important part of such a program is the congregation's willingness to allow those who minister with them to influence the ongoing development of the congregation's spirituality and charism.

What has been said for religious congregations also applies to clergy. In conducting continuing-education programs for diocesan clergy, we frequently ask the participants to share faith experiences. Often priests indicate that they have never shared faith with one another. One priest commented, "In the thirty years since my ordination, not one priest has ever asked me to share faith with him." After the initial resistance to sharing, there is generally an excitement and desire to continue. We encourage priests to share those experiences from the pulpit and to develop structures which allow those assembled to join them in faith sharing.

In working with groups who have had some success in their collaborative efforts, we have noticed one consistent characteristic: the ability to share faith. To share faith with another means revealing who God is for the person, and how God's presence is affecting his or her life. Questions such as "When have you been most aware of the presence of God in your life?" or "How have you discovered God through one another?" can help a group to share at this level. If a group is to become a community of disciples then the necessity of this faith dimension seems evident. There have been numerous occasions when we have invited ministering groups to engage in faith sharing, and the impact has been truly inspiring. The participants said that the experience helped to strengthen or to build trust, intimacy, understanding, acceptance, respect, and bonding. This type of communal prayer involves sharing at a personal level with community members or co-ministers; it means being vulnerable.

Many individuals are reluctant to share this most personal aspect of themselves. Their early formation discouraged such disclosure: faith was understood as a personal experience, not to be shared with others. However, every experience of God is a gift and all gifts, as we are told by St. Paul, are given for the sake of the community and to extend the reign of God. Experiences of God are meant to be shared for the edification of all.

The Conference of Major Superiors of Men conducted research designed to discover the conditions which help to foster the development of community. Their findings have relevance for collaborative ministry. They discovered that the most successful communities shared three characteristics. First, they had a common approach to the apostolate: they had discussed what they perceived as their common call, their common mission. Second, they were able to dialogue on a value level: they discussed issues of the heart. Third, they were able to share faith: they trusted one another with the most personal and vulnerable part of themselves, their experiences of God.

Creating a climate which helps to overcome fear and encourages sharing is essential. When people are able to share faith, they usually experience a corresponding ability to work more collaboratively with one another.

A Spirituality That Fits

Luke's gospel proclaims that the kingdom of God is within. If you wish to find God you must begin with an inward journey. Spiritualities which are indiscriminately imported from others or which are maintained beyond the time when they truly nurture the relationship are debilitating. God is revealed to each person at every moment of her or his life. God is a God of surprises, revealed in ways different from what might be expected. Failure to encounter God in a new way precludes growth in one's relationship with God.

Do you have a spirituality which fits you for who you are at this point in your life? Reflection on the following questions can assist in your discernment:

- Do I have a spirituality which fits me as male or female?
- Do I have a spirituality which fits my cultural background? (Irish, African-American, Hispanic, Italian, etc.)
- Do I have a spirituality which fits me for where I am developmentally? (As an adult do I continue to relate to God as if I were a child? Am I afraid to let go of a spirituality which was formerly nurturing but is no longer?)
- Do I have a spirituality which fits me for the particular circumstances in which I find myself?

Two examples show developing a spirituality to fit one's unique circumstances. A holy, dynamic, apostolic priest held a leadership position in our national government. He became terminally ill. We had the privilege of visiting him just before he died, and during the visit he shared, "I don't have a spirituality for dying." He went on to describe how he had a spirituality that fit him as an activist. But he knew that his former spirituality was no longer sustaining him in his present condition. In his wisdom he realized he had to discover God in his process of dying.

Another friend, with Parkinson's disease, pointed at his trembling hand and uttered, "When I can find God here, I'll have found God."

In *Seeds of Contemplation*, Thomas Merton wrote,

> Many poets are not poets for the same reason that many religious men are not saints. They never get around to being the particular poet or the particular monk they are intended to be by God. . . . They wear out their minds and bodies in hopeless endeavor to have somebody else's experience or write somebody else's poems.

Truly holy people discover God present in their unique reality. Bishop Hubbard also addressed this issue:

> Furthermore, the laity must strive to make the connection between faith and work, between weekend liturgy and weekday responsibilities, between seeing God's presence at the altar, at the desk, at the sink, on the farm, in the labor union hall, at the PTA meeting, in the political caucus and the legislative chamber (NCP).

The psycho-sexual level of development needs also to be integrated into one's spirituality, since it is part of the total person. The differences that occur during life's stages need to be integrated and expressed in one's spirituality.

For example, those in midlife often undergo a period of questioning, doubt, reassessment, and choice. This dynamic affects the whole of life including relationships with other persons and with God. When there is an awareness of this predictable dynamic, the experience is not so threatening, and individuals are better able to accept and to integrate the disquieting experience as part of normal growth. When the impact of this internal chaos on spiritual life is not recognized or accepted, however, internal turmoil can result.

It is helpful for persons experiencing midlife questioning to permit the questions to surface and be integrated, to grapple with the inevitable doubts, to investigate alternative options in terms of ministry, prayer, and lifestyle, and to move to a decision and to a commitment or recommitment. The need to move away from familiar prayer forms to different ones may surface. This is difficult to do because at midlife there is frequently a desire to retain the familiar which may provide security, but not growth.

Similarly, as people in ministry approach retirement, they often face a period of questioning, usually of a more specific nature:

- Have I been a good Christian?
- Will God be pleased with what I have been and done?
- Could/Should I have done more?
- What if there is no God?

Because these questions can be frightening, there is a tendency to avoid them. They need to be accepted and embraced as sent by God to give birth to a period of integrity, peace, and contentment in prayer life. If these questions are not brought to prayer, they often remain on the periphery of consciousness, leaving the questioner with a constant sense of disquietude and a lack of peace.

Developmental stages are experienced differently by each person. Even so, prayerful and encouraging support from others is helpful. The value of a communal, collaborative spirituality is that this support can be extended by others with whom one prays and ministers.

A Spirituality That Is Affective

Effective ministers are also affective ministers, meaning they exude a sense of passion. Passion exists when we give ourselves permission to experience the full range of emotions. Spirituality has not always been associated with the concept of passion. In fact, at a lecture given at the Georgetown Woodstock Center, Walter Burghardt, SJ, reflecting on the first eighty years of his life, commented "I regret that relatively little attention was given by retreat directors to the role of senses, to emotion and passion."

Collaborative ministers must be encouraged to cultivate a spirituality which allows them to integrate every aspect of their emotional life into their relationships with God. To show more clearly the impact of denying certain emotions, consider the following "single channel theory":

> Picture an emotional channel coursing through your body, similar to an artery which transports blood. This channel transports all the emotions. When a person is unable to accept an emotion, particularly one that is feared or considered negative, such as anger, it blocks the capacity to experience other emotions, such as love. Which emotions or feelings do you find most difficult to accept and integrate? Anger? Sexual feelings? Jealousy?

Anger, for instance, is often one of the more difficult emotions to accept and integrate into one's relationship with God. One of the holiest people we know is someone who is able, like the prophets of old, to vent her anger toward God. Because she can accept and express her anger toward God, she also has a very personal, passionate, loving relationship with God.

The recognition and integration of feelings and emotions is part of human development. Their acceptance and expression are avenues through which a person grows into maturity. Some people, however, limit the range of emotions they allow themselves in their relationship with God. They may permit themselves, for example, to express their affection, but fear may prevent them from recognizing and accepting their feelings of anger toward God.

Collaborative ministry brings people together in numerous ways and may trigger a variety of feelings and emotions. It is imperative that people in ministry become more comfortable with their emotions, bringing them into every aspect of their lives, including their spirituality. Inability to recognize and claim feelings will undoubtedly hamper people in ministering collaboratively and in their spiritual growth.

A Spirituality That Integrates Failure

Many Christians have grown up with a theology and spirituality of perfectionism. This is an ideal reinforced by our competitive culture. Perfectionism is an obstacle not only to collaboration, but also to developing a balanced spirituality. When perfectionists become aware of their limitations, they may become critical or judgmental toward themselves, others, and life in general. They find it extremely difficult to appreciate their own goodness and spirituality when they confront the inevitable failures that are a part of life, not to mention those that are part of collaborative ministry. These are the people who find it too threatening to their self-esteem to risk sharing faith with others. They fear that in the process of sharing, the others will become aware of their lack of perfection.

One solution is to help people move from a spirituality of perfection to a spirituality of failure. They need to know that they are good, spiritual people, even when they fail, that God can be found in failure perhaps more easily than in success. People who have been reared on the injunction to "be perfect as your heavenly Father is perfect" (Mt 5:48) usually find it difficult to integrate failure into their spirituality. These ministers need encouragement and affirmation to become more accepting of their own brokenness.

An insightful friend, when asked what he would do if he were in charge of a ministry formation program responded, "Create a program in which they feel free to fail." Emotional and spiritual growth take place when a person can fail without losing self-esteem. On the other hand, when a person is protected from failure and is formed in the belief that failure is intolerable, there is little preparation for integrating the failures in life and ministry into spirituality.

During a workshop we were conducting for social justice ministers, the participants were asked to chart their successes and failures in ministry. Those who were able to accept their perceived failures also recognized the acceptance of these failures as times of spiritual growth. Those who had difficulty accepting failure often became fixated in their spiritual development at these times.

Jesus is the model for all spirituality, yet his life was a series of apparent failures. St. Paul wrote about his own failures, proclaiming how he often did the things that he did not want to do. His life demonstrates how willingness to constructively accept failure can lead to new depths of spirituality.

Failure is a reality of life, especially for those who risk trying new things. Coping constructively with failure creates a freedom that allows ministers to share with others, especially those with whom they minister.

Conclusion

In this chapter we have shared some elements of a spirituality for collaborative ministry. You may or may not agree with our insights and conclusions. Regardless, as you read through the sections we hope you engage in this simple process. First, reflect on your beliefs about a spirituality for collaborative ministry. Second, identify some individuals whom you perceive as living a truly spiritual life. Engage in dialogue with them about their spirituality. From the reflection and conversations, elements of a spirituality for collaborative ministry will emerge.

Reflection/Discussion Questions

1. What do I believe are the elements of a spirituality for collaborative ministry?

2. In examining my own spirituality, what are aspects that I need to reassess in light of current realities?

3. In what ways would I like to see my spirituality:
   —move to compassionate action?
   —encompass forgiveness?
   —be more reflective?
   —be more shared?
   —fit the person who I am?
   —be affective?
   —integrate failure?

7

Group Leadership

Collaborative ministry calls forth attitudes, behaviors, and skills different from those needed in the past. Even when the concept of collaborative ministry is attractive and desirable, ministers may experience difficulty in developing a more collaborative style because they have not developed the requisite skills.

Unless ministers have a degree of competency in the skills demanded by a more relational form of ministry, even the best designed process will not enable collaboration. We believe that the ability to lead a group is among the most important skills required. Since collaboration is never an isolated event but occurs within the context of a group, the skill of leadership is an essential one to develop.

Some people in ministry presume that they possess the skill of leading a group even when there has been no formal training in this area. Among some there is a misconception that group leadership is a natural talent acquired with entrance into ministry. Nothing could be further from the truth. Groups are complex organisms, and group leadership demands a level of trained competency. Group leadership should be an integral aspect of the formal training in all ministry formation.

Today there is adequate training for the growth and development of individuals who wish to participate in ministry. The same attention is often not afforded to furthering group growth and development. Given the fact that people in ministry work with a number of groups, we would hope that this void will be corrected in future ministry training programs.

Jesuit-psychiatrist, Angelo D'Agostino, who trained the authors, realized that present theology concentrates on the development of *communio* and communion. People are saved and healed in a context of community. As a psychiatrist he knew that the same dynamics which effect every group are also present in every community. He concluded that it would be imperative that any leader in the communal, collaborative church be trained in understanding these dynamics and learning how to provide effective leadership.

The written word can never substitute adequately for leadership skills acquired in a formal training program. However, the information presented in this chapter can help to lay the groundwork for developing greater skill in group leadership.

This chapter will briefly discuss Jesus as a model of a collaborative leader, present a model for understanding the normal development that occurs in groups, provide a leadership paradigm for facilitating and leading groups, and offer additional principles regarding group leadership.

Jesus as a Model for the Collaborative Leader

The style of leadership is related to one's image of Jesus as a leader. Who is your Jesus? Is he the Jesus of Matthew 9, who seems to be almost obsessively responding to the needs of all: a paralytic, the father of a dead girl, a woman with a hemorrhage, two blind men, and a mute possessed by a demon? It comes as no surprise that at the end of this chapter, Jesus implores his disciples to pray to the "harvest master" to send additional "laborers." If this very active Jesus is your image of leadership, you may become overwhelmed by the incessant demands of responding personally to the needs of each individual.

Perhaps your model is Jesus as a collaborative leader. This is the Jesus who from the very beginning of his public ministry gathered a group of disciples to minister *with* him. He taught, formed, and instilled in them a sense of mission. Jesus, the collaborative leader, sent the disciples in pairs into ministry even before they were perfectly formed. He was there to receive them when they returned from their missionary journeys, and he helped them to reflect on their successes and failures. Jesus was the secure collaborative leader who could return to his Father and could leave his disciples to continue the mission, even though they were far from completely formed. Jesus knew that they had the Holy Spirit to guide and lead them. Is this your model of ministry? Are you like the collaborative Jesus who is the paradigm for all collaborative leaders?

Growth as a Group

An important aspect of effective group leadership is the realization that groups progress through a developmental process, not unlike that of individuals. When leaders attend to that developmental reality, they can be effective in furthering the growth and development of the group, and ultimately the mission of the group. Every group has the capacity to be life-giving and constructive, or life-draining and destructive. One principal factor in determining whether the group becomes destructive or constructive is the degree to which the leader and members understand the dynamics through which groups proceed.

There are numerous models of group development. Angelo D'Agostino, SJ, mentioned earlier, served as a psychiatric consultant to the Peace Corps. D'Agostino identified the four stages which can also characterize groups and organizations attempting to be collaborative.

In the first stage, characterized by *enthusiasm, excitement,* and *anxiety*, expect to observe a minimum of collaboration. Marked by an initial fervor or even an emotional high, leaders tend to do everything by themselves. At this time they are not usually focused on being collaborative. Their energy is often expended in locating a personal comfort zone. Even though they may be unaware of it, their psychological focus is directed toward the reinforcement of a somewhat fragile self-esteem. Because they are consciously or unconsciously seeking the approval and esteem of others, leaders tend to do too much for those they serve. The anxiety, of course, augments this vulnerability. They are unable to focus on the giftedness of others. There is a propensity to work individually rather than seeking ways to work collaboratively. At this stage, the leader of a group tends to be self-absorbed, rather than collaborative.

The second phase, *disillusionment,* can be a difficult stage for many leaders. The idealism which propels them into frenetic activity often does not produce the desired results or responses from those they serve. They begin to face the reality that their dedication does not produce results commensurate with the energy expended. It is a difficult and, sometimes, depressing time. Collaboration is often the furthest thought from the leader's mind. This is a time characterized by hyper-criticalness of the organization and of its leaders. This defensive behavior masks frustration, disappointment, disillusionment, and diminished self-esteem.

The third stage, a time of *decision* and *discernment,* is a crucial one for most leaders. Depending on how they resolve the disillusionment of Stage 2, they opt either for a recommitment to the reality of the group, or they choose to withdraw. The withdrawal can be either a psychological and emotional one, or an actual, physical withdrawal. They may begin to perform their ministries as mere functionaries or they may choose to terminate their commitment. If they opt for the recommitment, this is the time to foster the ideal of collaboration. There has been adequate experience to convince them that their isolated efforts will only produce minimal results. It becomes apparent that collaborative ministry is both the desired approach and the gospel approach.

The final phase, *termination,* is important both for the leaders and for those they minister to. Times of "moving on" are ideal times for the leaders and the group to reflect on the implications of a death-resurrection theology. Termination can be an emotionally volatile time for all involved. Reflecting on this experience and talking about it can lead to new personal and theological insights. Individuals who do not process their experiences of termination tend to be held hostage by the unfinished business of incomplete grieving. In some cases the failure to complete the grieving process connected with terminations precludes the willingness to enter into future collaboration.

Awareness of these or similar stages can assist Christian leaders in understanding the personal struggle of becoming more collaborative. In *Building Community: Christian, Caring, Vital*, we presented a developmental model of groups which guides our work in collaborative efforts. The eight-stage model begins with attention to the group's way of dealing with the endings, and also follows a group through predictable, developmental stages. The next section offers an overview of our paradigm for group leadership.

A Basic Model for Group Leadership

The "rolodex method" for group leadership derives its name from the device which sits on many office desks. A rolodex serves as a quick reference for locating important data such as telephone numbers or addresses. The device consists of a series of file cards of information placed on a rotating shaft. A particular address, for example, is quickly located by merely rotating the files to the desired card. Mentally picture a rolodex containing just six cards with each card listing one function for the group leader:

1. to create a climate of safety;
2. to encourage interaction among the members;
3. to adhere to the task established by the group;
4. to direct the group toward the purpose;
5. to intervene when the dynamics prevent group progress;
6. to evaluate the progress of the group.

The leader follows the cards sequentially and focuses on one card at a time. When the leader is satisfied that the first function has been completed, the next card is flipped and attention is focused on that particular function. This rolodex method is a simple and easy way for group leaders to visualize their primary functions. When leading a group, some people have found it helpful to actually write the six functions on index cards which they place in front of them during the group sessions. More information on each function follows.

Creating a Safe Climate

Until there is a feeling of safety, it is impossible for the members of a group to apply themselves to their task. Since groups are by nature anxiety-producing, the energy of the participants easily becomes diverted to self-protection. Membership in any group often confronts a person with numerous uncertainties and insecurities:

- How will these people treat me?
- Will I be accepted?
- How will I be challenged to change in this group?
- Will this group threaten my self-esteem?

There is usually a greater sense of control in one-to-one situations than in group settings, and this feeling of less control can compound the anxiety level for some people.

The first function of the leader, therefore, is to create a climate in which everyone feels safe enough to share or to remain silent. If the climate is safe, the group can grow and achieve its purpose; if the climate is unsafe, the growth of the group and its members will be severely impeded.

There are a number of ways to build a climate of safety. The leader can put the group at ease by acknowledging the anxiety and asking what would help lessen it. Identifying and acknowledging the feeling as a universal experience reduces anxiety.

We discourage the round-robin approach in which the leader asks each person to respond in turn. The effect of this approach on some people is that anxiety increases, and they mentally busy themselves formulating an acceptable response. Since their attention is directed toward their own response, they are unable to listen to previous speakers. After speaking, they are often still not free to listen because they are now evaluating what they have said, deciding how it could have been said better, or assessing the reactions of others to their words.

One way of creating a safe climate is to assist the group in clarifying its expectations. This is particularly important in the early stages of group life. The leader can ask herself or himself:

- What can be expected of this group?
- What is expected of each member?
- What can be realistically expected of the leader?

The time spent in clarification reduces ambiguity, which is one of the primary causes of anxiety.

The leader needs to be sensitive, especially in the initial meetings, to anything within the group which may threaten a person's self-esteem. When certain threatening or aggressive behaviors are allowed to occur without any leader intervention, the members usually feel fearful and vulnerable. Scapegoating is one example of such behavior. One member or a small group of members is unilaterally blamed for any of the perceived problems in the group. Any type of behavior which puts down another, either directly or indirectly, can erode the level of safety. Most people experience a lessening of self-esteem when their person or their ideas are attacked. Others experience this when a suggestion or thought they offer to the group receives no response. Leaders who are sensitive to these dynamics can be more assertive in intervening in ways that help everyone understand what is happening. Of course the leader must be careful not to put people down in the process.

A further way of assuring safety is to encourage the group to develop an explicit contract regarding confidentiality. Most people hesitate to share in any setting where what they said for the group may be repeated to others outside the group. To assure confidentiality, the group members need to explicitly agree to certain conditions. The following questions can be addressed and responded to:

- Can the substance of this meeting be repeated to others?
- What, if anything, that is said within the group can be told outside the group?
- Are certain issues that the group discusses not to leave the group?

Problems regarding confidentiality are often problems of communication. Each person has a belief about what constitutes confidentiality. The internal belief has to be made explicit, and the group members must reach some agreement about their mutual expectations regarding confidentiality.

The leader should introduce the topic of confidentiality at the first meeting and again whenever new members are added. Once there is common agreement about expectations regarding confidentiality, everyone can be held accountable for honoring them. Anyone who believes that the agreement has been broken has the responsibility to bring this concern immediately to the group. A concern about a breach of confidentiality should take precedence over anything else on the agenda. Until confidence is restored, the group will not feel free to share on other topics.

Finally, leaders must learn to listen for symbolic language in groups. Group discussions which focus on people outside the group who cannot be trusted, for example, usually indicate that there is a feeling of distrust in the group itself. The alert leader can take this opportunity to check whether the feeling of distrust is felt toward the entire group or only particular members.

Encouraging Interaction Within the Group

When the climate within the group is safe enough that the members feel free to participate, the leader can assess more closely the dynamics of the interaction taking place. It is in the early stages that a group tends to direct conversation toward the leader. The leader's task is to encourage dialogue among the group members. For some leaders this is not an easy task. Difficulty may stem from the leader's anxiety or need to be in constant control of the group or to be the perennial center of attention. Since the leader may be unaware of those needs and the resulting behavior, supervision and consultation may be necessary to help a leader recognize and change behavior which is group-destructive. Any group leader must be convinced that there is greater value in what the members share with each other than in what he or she says. Unless this is truly a conviction, no change will occur in leadership style.

As mentioned earlier, one way to assess the leader-centeredness of a group is to examine the leader's energy level. When the leader leaves a session exhausted, it is usually a clear indication that he or she has done the work of the group. It is imperative that leaders question their beliefs regarding the potential of the group and its individual members. Do they really believe that the group members have the gifts among themselves to accomplish the tasks they have set? If yes, then do they allow the group to exercise its capability? When a group feels responsible for what has been accomplished, the group experiences its own potency. This enhances the self-esteem of the members and gives new vitality to the group.

Group-centeredness can be fostered in different ways. First, the leader's simple verbal encouragement to talk to one another can shift the focus of attention. For example, the leader can refrain from answering questions which are directly addressed to him or her. It is a temptation for leaders to presume that the group is most interested in their opinions. However, as we have discovered from experience, once a leader suggests that the group first share their responses to the question, the group rarely returns to ask the leader's opinion. This can be a humbling revelation for the leader, but it is a valuable lesson for effectively fulfilling the role of group leader.

Our final recommendation involves behavior which might initially appear as the antithesis of good ministry. In a one-to-one ministry situation it is imperative to direct full attention to the other person. This can be communicated in many ways, but usually it means looking directly at the person and conveying complete interest in everything that is said. Leaders who assume this same stance in group situations discover that it is counterproductive. If the leader rivets attention on the person speaking, then that person, in turn, focuses on the leader to the exclusion of the rest of the group. Rather, it is more effective if the leader develops the self-discipline to divert his or her gaze from the speaker, perhaps by looking around the group. When the leader acts in this way, the speaker generally addresses the group rather than just the leader. For those trained for one-to-one ministry this approach is uncomfortable. The transition to a group-centered approach takes much practice.

Adhering to the Task

Once the members of the group feel secure and are talking with one another, the next function on the rolodex is to examine what the group is discussing. During the initial meeting the group should develop a contract which addresses certain aspects:

- What is the purpose of the group?
- What is the task of the group?
- How frequently will the group meet?
- What is the length of time of the meetings?
- What are the expectations of the members and of the leader?
- What is the policy regarding confidentiality?
- What is the method for including new members?
- What expectations does the group have regarding absences?

The essential element of this verbal contract is the statement of what the group hopes to achieve—its purpose. The group's purpose provides the foundation for all other aspects of the contract. The group's purpose expresses what the group hopes to achieve together, while its task defines the way in which it will be done. For example, a particular staff might decide that its purpose is "to develop a working relationship as staff which will assist each person to be more effective in ministry." The accompanying task might be to meet to share what each person is doing in ministry and to hear suggestions which might increase each member's effectiveness. Once the group has clearly defined its purpose and task, the role of the leader is clear: to determine if the group is doing what it has agreed to do. Ordinarily, whenever the group discusses irrelevant topics, the leader challenges the group to return to its task.

During the course of a group's life, it sometimes becomes necessary to renegotiate the task. This can happen when the group realizes that there are other more important or pressing issues to be discussed. For example, a staff may realize that it is more important to discuss the group members' feelings of loss and anger over the pastor's upcoming transfer than the agreed-upon task. If the group consents to the change, then the leader has the responsibility to hold it accountable to the newly defined task. Later we will discuss the leader's function when the group is resistant to the task at hand.

Moving the Group Toward the Purpose

If the group members feel safe enough to talk with one another and are adhering to the task, the leader has been doing a good job. Some groups continue at the level of discussion, but accomplish nothing. At this point the leader flips to the fourth rolodex card and focuses on helping the group move toward its purpose. Most groups fail for two reasons: (1) there is no clearly articulated purpose or (2) the purpose is neglected as an ongoing criteria for evaluating the group's progress. This is true for any group, whether organization, community, team, parish, or diocese. Although the primary efforts of a group should be directed toward achieving its purpose, there is a tendency in most groups to divert energy into many extraneous issues. When a group reaches a level of productive discussion, the leader must challenge the group to take action which will move it toward the established purpose.

In the example given above, the purpose of the staff was to develop a working relationship which would assist each member to be more effective in ministry. Given this purpose, the leader needs to raise questions which encourage the group to make decisions about how the members will personally and collectively use what they discover in the discussions to improve their effectiveness.

At this point it is easy for the leader to become overly complacent. Satisfied that the group is talking and is at peace, the leader may neglect to notice if there is any commensurate action accompanying the talk.

Facilitating the Process

The term "process" simply refers to what is happening in a group. It is this dynamic which demands the greatest skill on the part of the leader. Things happen during the life of any group which draw away energy and attention from the task at hand and focus on something which has become more important to the group. The group members may show an emotional response, the cause of which is not clearly identifiable, which becomes the focal point for their energy. When this dynamic occurs, the group is unable to focus on the original purpose. Either directly or indirectly it focuses its attention and emotion on the new, often unconscious issue.

The following story shows the dynamics that may arise in a group.

> A social worker in a government agency was directed to lead a group of prospective adopting parents. The purpose of the group was to help prepare the couples to be better adopting parents, and the task was to discuss their feelings and concerns. The social worker's concern was his inability to keep the group focused on its task as the number of available babies was limited, and only a few of the couples would receive a child. In addition, it was the social worker who would ultimately determine which couples would be selected. Despite the social worker's attempts, the couples resisted discussing the articulated task. Instead, they spent the entire meeting talking about the local football team.

This story is an example of a group in flight. The process involved their fears about any self-disclosure which could ultimately affect the social worker's decision. The fear was so intense that the group's energy was diverted onto a much safer topic. Once the social worker identified and named for the group what was happening, the members were able to talk about these fears and the situation in which they found themselves. Consequently, the contract was renegotiated and the group was then able to pursue a more realistic task.

Process usually refers to the feelings and/or fears of the group members. Anytime the process interferes with the progress of the group, the leader's function is to recognize the fact that something is happening and to encourage the group to deal with the process before returning to the task. Due to the presence of resistance, numerous leader interventions may be required to force the group to acknowledge and to deal with the process. Because dealing with an emotional process is usually terribly threatening to a group, the members may unconsciously collude in order to avoid accepting and facing the reality of the present situation.

Some leaders become so process-conscious that they focus exclusively on the process to the exclusion of the task. A general rule for leaders is to focus on the process only when it obstructs the task, and only for as long as is needed. The leader may not always be able to correctly identify the cause of the behavior, but a general comment to the members that something is interfering with their ability to function adequately is just as important and can help the group explore its resistance.

Often, when a leader attempts to encourage the group to deal with the process, the members respond by uniting in a concerted effort to "kill the leader." This is a defensive behavior which protects the group when it feels threatened. It is important that leaders be strong enough to pursue the process despite the group's anger. Leaders who are fearful of anger, conflict, and confrontation can easily align themselves with the group, and this behavior can condemn the group to failure.

Evaluating the Meeting

The final function of the leader is to help the group evaluate its progress. Though important, this function is often bypassed even by very good leaders, possibly because it poses a potential threat to the leader's self-esteem.

The preferable way to evaluate is to engage the members directly in this process since the members are in the best position to determine the group's progress. This can be accomplished by regularly allotting time for "post-grouping." Post-grouping consists of reserving about ten minutes at the end of the meeting for the group members to become detached from the content they were discussing and to focus on the process and progress that occurred. Since the post-grouping is not meant to evolve into another meeting, the leader should be careful to limit the time. A typical post-grouping session might pose any of the following questions:

- How safe did you feel at this meeting?
- Is there anything which would have made you feel even safer?
- Did anything occur during this session which either contributed to or detracted from a climate of safety?

- What one thing was most helpful to you? (Be specific.)
- What would you like to have seen happen that did not?
- During this meeting did we talk about what we agreed to? Did it help us move closer to our purpose?
- Was there anything which occurred that you wanted to comment on but didn't? Would you be willing to make that comment now?
- What would you suggest for making our meetings better in the future?

Often during the post-grouping, members who have been extremely quiet during the session provide valuable insights on the dynamics of the meeting. It is also during this time that the leader may be able to uncover the reason why certain insights or reactions were not voiced and can encourage the members to take more initiative in the future. The use of the above or similar questions allows the members to evaluate and to assume more responsibility for the success of the meetings.

Some Hints on Leadership

While our major focus in this chapter has been on a theoretical model for group leadership, we would also like offer thirteen suggestions (see Table 7.1) for group leaders that focus on necessary attitudes and behaviors.

Table 7.1	*Suggestions for Leaders*
	1. Examine your own beliefs.
	2. Think group.
	3. Focus on both the content and the process.
	4. Prepare for meetings.
	5. Reflect on all meetings.
	6. Trust your feelings.
	7. Be direct and gentle.
	8. Clarify and summarize.
	9. Rarely bring closure.
	10. Make group interventions.
	11. Avoid the role of teacher and preacher.
	12. Develop a sense of timing.
	13. Seek consultation and supervision.

1. Examine your own beliefs. Do you believe that groups have as much potential for growth as they do for destruction? Testing what you believe about groups in general is a good starting point. One belief which we encourage is the leader's basic attitude toward a group. As part of facilitator training for a national meeting, the presenters posed a question, "Do you see the group as allies or adversaries?" When the leader perceives the group in an adversarial way, it can provoke a defensive or hostile reaction from the group. Conversely, when the leader feels and communicates a positive attitude forming an alliance with the group, the group responds more positively. Before entering into a group, leaders can benefit from reflecting on what they feel and how they image the group. When they are feeling anxious and defensive, time should be spent refocusing. The mind projects only what the individual tells it. So leaders choose which way they will visualize the group.

2. Think group. One way to do this is to imagine that you are looking at the group through trifocal lenses. The first lens focuses on what is happening to each individual. The second lens focuses on the dynamics which occur between individuals within the group. (Does A respond every time B talks? Does C always agree or disagree with everything that D says? Does the entire group tend to overestimate whatever E says? Does it underestimate any contributions from F?) Through the third lens of the trifocals, the leader focuses on the group as a whole. For most ministers it is easy to view a group through the perspective of the first two lenses. It is the third lens which presents problems, especially for those who have been trained in a one-to-one counseling approach. A leader's ability to view the group as a whole does not usually come naturally, but requires training and practice. This perspective allows the leader to see beyond individuals and observe the behavior that is reflective of the group. The leader can ask questions such as:

- What is now the major theme of this group?
- How is the group permitting or encouraging what is happening?
- How is the behavior of one individual expressing a belief or attitude of the whole group?

A leader's ability to perceive through this third lens is normally acquired and sharpened as a result of training and ongoing supervision. This capacity to "think group" is a distinguishing characteristic of effective group leaders.

3. Focus on both the content and the process. Most ministers have been trained to concentrate on hearing what is being said and may miss the more important message that is being communicated indirectly in the process. Training helps a leader alternate between hearing the direct communication and what Virginia Satir calls the "metacommunication," the communication which is expressed indirectly through allusion, symbol, or nonverbal behavior. Preoccupation with the verbal message interferes with the ability to hear the unspoken message.

4. Prepare for meetings. A good leader prepares for a meeting by taking time to review what happened at the last meeting, reflect on what has happened in the interim which might affect the upcoming meeting, and anticipate what issues, conflicts, or dynamics are likely to occur at the meeting. The success of the meeting is usually in direct proportion to the amount of time the leader has taken to prepare for it.

5. Reflect on all meetings. In addition to the post-grouping which was mentioned above, we recommend that leaders take time immediately after the conclusion of a meeting to reflect on what has just transpired. Given the complexity of groups, leaders can never be fully aware of everything that has happened during a meeting. By taking some emotional distance, a leader may better understand the dynamics that occurred during the meeting. These and similar questions can help in this reflection:

- What was I feeling during the meeting and what might this feeling indicate?
- Was there any time when I was feeling particularly uncomfortable or fearful?
- What could I have done differently to make the meeting better?

6. Trust your feelings. Among the group leaders that we have trained, many have been sensitive to the emotional tone during a given meeting. However, we find that people generally need encouragement to believe in their own powers of perception. Frequently during a meeting the leader will experience feelings, such as anxiety or anger. These feelings, though not yet verbalized, are indicative of the emotional climate operating within the group. Trusting those feelings and thinking about their cause can help a leader decide the best action to take with the group.

Leaders need to identify the source of their feelings. They may arise from causes unrelated to the group; for example, the leader may walk into the meeting feeling sad or angry because of a recent encounter. However, if the leader enters the group feeling cheerful and during the course of the meeting begins to feel a sense of sadness with no apparent cause for this shift in feeling, the group may be unconsciously conveying this feeling of sadness to the leader.

7. *Be direct and gentle.* We have become increasingly convinced that the combination of direct honesty and gentle compassion produces the best results in working with groups. Many ministers are more comfortable with gentleness than they are with directness. The best group leaders are those who are able to integrate both qualities into their style of leadership. Leadership behavior which is both direct and gentle helps the members of the group feel safe and have confidence in the leader.

8. *Clarify and summarize.* One of the best group leaders we encountered was a man who possessed an almost uncanny ability to listen to a group for five minutes in one session and then accurately predict what would occur in the group for a series of sessions thereafter. One might expect that his leadership of a group would include many brilliant and insightful interventions. Instead, ninety percent of his interventions were clarifying comments and questions.

We, too, have found that clarifications, that is, occasional short summaries of what has transpired, are helpful to participants. Leaders are well-advised to emphasize clarifying summaries and to avoid seemingly brilliant group interventions (see number ten, below) which usually only impress the person making them while confusing the group members.

9. *Rarely bring closure.* There are a rare few times when it is appropriate and necessary to bring closure to discussions. Yet some ministers have a propensity to put closure on *everything*. In many church-affiliated groups it is often beneficial to have people leave the meetings with some questions unanswered.

The absence of closure can force people to continue their reflection between meetings and can encourage them to expand their thinking.

10. Make group interventions. There are two basic approaches to group work: to focus on the individual in the group or to focus on the group as a whole. We believe that groups are more effective when the leader addresses interventions toward the entire group rather than any individual. Most interventions which can be directed at an individual can be expanded to encompass the entire group. The following example illustrates a group intervention.

During a staff meeting, a staff member asked how to deal with a feeling of intense loneliness. The other staff members quickly and almost obsessively offered advice which was of a highly impersonal and somewhat condescending nature. After the advice-giving had continued for a while, the leader asked if the staff member who raised the question was the only one who had experienced loneliness since the responses had not indicated that it had ever been a problem for the others. Slowly the other members of the staff honestly and compassionately began sharing some of their own struggles with loneliness. The leader's group intervention had moved them from focusing on one person to seeing the issue of loneliness as a universal experience.

11. Avoid the role of teacher or preacher. We have identified three categories of professionals who seem to have the most difficulty adjusting to the role of group leader or facilitator: persons trained for individual counseling, teachers, and preachers. The latter two groups have a tendency to always have an answer or solution for any problem or issue the group raises. Many teachers and preachers find it difficult to enable others and facilitate groups. Their style of leadership curtails the group from discovering solutions. As noted before, people trained as individual counselors often have difficulty in focusing on the group as a whole. It is our observation that group members who revert to teaching or preaching are the least influential members of the group. After awhile the group seems to "tune out" when these people begin responding. The same can be said of those who intervene too frequently. Those who intervene less frequently usually exert a greater influence on the group.

12. Develop a sense of timing. The concept of timing in working with groups is one of the most difficult areas for group leaders to learn, and also for instructors to convey. It is common for those learning to work with groups to experience the frustration of leaving a meeting knowing that there were moments when an intervention should have been made. However, by the time they had worked through the mental gymnastics of deciding on the perfect intervention, the group had moved to a different level or topic, and the intervention was no longer appropriate or relevant. The secret is to realize when an intervention is needed and to be willing to make an intervention which may be less than perfect or even completely off target. If the intervention is made in a way that encourages the participants to disagree and/or grapple with what is happening in the group, it will usually prove valuable. Again, by taking time after the meeting for reflection, the leader can often determine what would have been a more appropriate intervention and be better prepared when a similar situation occurs in the future. Perhaps more important than the "right" intervention is a sense of the opportune moment to intervene and the initiative to act at all.

13. Seek consultation or supervision. Ministry is perhaps the only helping profession which does not require continuing education, consultation, or supervision. This is particularly dangerous for persons whose ministries focus primarily on individual or group counseling. Meeting regularly with a person or group who will evaluate and critique their work helps ministers be more effective and can reduce the possibility of their harming the people they are attempting to serve.

Conclusion

Collaborative ministry, by its very nature, involves participation in and leadership of groups. Group dynamics occur in all groups, including faith-sharing and ministry groups. The more that the members and leaders understand the dynamics of group, the more likely it is that the groups will be life-giving for both the members and the mission. Unfortunately, only a minority of ministers have had formal training in working with groups.

Reflection/Discussion Questions

1. What specific, in-depth training have I received in group dynamics and group leadership? How and where can I get further training?

2. How do I view Jesus as a leader? How does that perception of him influence my leadership style?

3. At what stage of D'Agostino's developmental model (pages 105-106) is my group?

4. How can I utilize the "rolodex" model for group leadership?

5. Which recommendations regarding group leadership are most important for me to develop?

8

Conflict

Although conflict is inevitable in a collaborative setting, it is by no means easy to address. In fact ministers in almost every culture where we have worked admit their difficulty in dealing with conflict. Research in the United States (e.g., National Opinion Research Center, Murnion, and Nigren Ukeritis) has indicated that clergy, laity, and religious all have difficulty with conflict.

In discussing collaboration the United States Conference of Catholic Bishops emphasized that if collaboration is to become a reality in the church, attention must be paid to developing the skill of conflict.

> Rather than avoid conflict, the wise community will ensure that some of its members have the training and skills to help the group deal positively with conflict so that it becomes a means for learning and growth (FWD, p. 20).

Although most ministers today acknowledge the need to develop effective conflict skills, they find doing so extremely threatening.

Role-playing is often the most successful approach to teaching this skill. By enacting a typical conflict situation the participants can identify the cause of the conflict, observe the dynamics that transpired during the role-play, and make recommendations to reduce, manage, or resolve the conflict. However, the medium of writing does not allow teaching through role-play, so we must settle for a less dynamic and effective way to communicate these skills.

Beliefs About Conflict

Personal beliefs about conflict and its appropriateness in the life of a Christian or in the Christian community make conflict situations difficult for many in ministry. The following list provides ways to explore one's personal beliefs about conflict.

1. Conflict is inevitable in the Christian community. The humorous statement, "Wherever two or more are gathered in his name, there will be conflict," contains more truth than most would care to admit. Whenever two people come together with their unique histories, needs, and values, there is likely to be a clash of histories, needs, and values. Therefore, it is no surprise to discover conflict among good, Christian people. On the contrary, its absence should cause suspicion. When conflict does not emerge in a relationship or in a group, it is often an indication that the conflict has been repressed or suppressed.

Sometime in history, a myth developed exempting religious people from the universal human phenomenon called conflict. While the existence of conflict among God-fearing people might scandalize some Christians, its presence indicates life and humanness in the church. In fact, conflict has always been present in the church. The gospels, for instance, show the apostles in conflict over who had the closest relationship with the Lord. Perhaps there would be greater willingness to accept the inevitability of conflict in the Christian community if it were seen as a normal rather than a deviant phenomenon.

2. Conflict is never easy. Although conflict is inevitable, it is not our intention to present an image of dealing with conflict which is unrealistic or "Pollyanna-ish." Quite the contrary, conflict is usually difficult, often messy, and frequently painful. While reading about conflict will not remove the difficulty, messiness, or pain, we believe that through increased understanding there will be a greater willingness to deal directly with inevitable conflicts and a better readiness to manage or resolve them.

3. There is a difference between conflict management and conflict resolution. Many people approach conflict with the desire to resolve it, remove it, and reinstate harmony. To expect to achieve this goal in all circumstances is unrealistic. While conflict resolution is possible, conflict management is often more realistic. Managing conflict means being able to live and work together even though the source of conflict has not been eliminated. An example will help to clarify the distinction between conflict management and conflict resolution.

When a certain parish council addressed the issue of the presence of statues in the sanctuary, two "camps" immediately formed. One group felt strongly that there were too many statues in the sanctuary and that their presence detracted from the celebration of the liturgy. The other group felt equally strongly that the statues should remain since they had been there for years and some had even been donated by the grandparents of the members of the group.

Given such a scenario, the chances are good that the final decision will not resolve the conflict to everyone's satisfaction. Many strong feelings will remain. As a Christian community, the parish council must decide how to deal with the resultant feelings in a way that attends to the pain and hurt while continuing to work together to further the kingdom. In this instance the conflict has not been resolved but merely managed.

On the other hand, the same parish council may be planning a parish renewal. Two ministerial groups are being considered to conduct the program. A number of council meetings are dedicated to discussing the relative merits of the two groups. Some council members favor one group; other members feel strongly that the other group is more suitable for the parish at this time. Over the course of the meetings the whole parish council decides that while either team would be a good choice, the first team is preferred at this time. This is a case of conflict resolution.

While we have used the example of a parish council, the application is the same for two individuals, a community, or any other groups attempting to work collaboratively.

4. Conflict which is confronted and managed or confronted and resolved leads to group cohesion. There are two important points underlying this belief. First, conflict has been confronted and not avoided. Second, as a result of the encounter, something positive (conflict management or conflict resolution) has happened. Only when these two conditions have been met can the group achieve cohesiveness. Until this occurs, the group is loosely-related individuals who lack any real binding relationships. There is no community and no collaboration.

For too many people the norm within the Christian community is peace at any price, regardless of what that price may be. Somewhere in the recesses of the individual and collective mind is a menacing superego which reiterates a dictum—good Christians never fight—that affects behavior. The result is an unspoken collusion to deny the existence of any conflict. When it becomes apparent that the conflict can no longer be denied, then all energy is diverted to avoid dealing with the conflict. We are convinced that collaboration is only possible when individuals have the courage to acknowledge, confront, and deal directly with conflict.

Another dynamic that often operates in the Christian community is the withdrawal that occurs when it becomes evident that a conflict is not going to simply disappear. The natural tendency is to give up immediately when the pain and messiness of conflict become apparent. However, in order to create Christian community there must be a willingness for the sake of the gospel to step beyond this natural reaction and to continue dealing with the conflict until management or resolution occurs.

Following conflict through to a point of management or resolution gives a group a sense of potency. The members realize that they possess the ability to deal with conflict without destruction of themselves or others. Failure to work conflict through to this point produces the opposite experience. An intensely debilitating feeling of impotency results from the belief that the group is unable to ever deal effectively with conflict, and behavior then becomes controlled by this fantasy.

5. Conflict which is not managed or resolved leads to pain for the individual and death to any collaborative efforts. Dealing with conflict leads to potency; failure to do so results in apathy and tension which are obstacles to collaboration. While collaboration is the desire to join others in uniting gifts for the sake of the mission, apathy is the antithesis of collaboration.

Conflict inevitably produces tension. People who work and minister together, yet choose not to acknowledge and handle the conflicts that arise, will create a tension-filled climate that prevents collaboration.

Throughout this section we have introduced a number of potential beliefs about conflict. Review the beliefs from Table 8.1 and compare the statements with your own beliefs.

Table 8.1

Beliefs About Conflict
Which of the following beliefs facilitate your ability to deal constructively with conflict? Which beliefs impede your ability to deal constructively with conflict?
- Conflict is inevitable in a Christian community.
- Religious people do not experience conflict.
- Conflict among Christians is a scandal.
- Conflict is a sign of life.
- Conflict is difficult, messy, and painful.
- There is a difference between conflict resolution and conflict management.
- Conflict when confronted and managed or resolved leads to group cohesion.
- Peace at any price.
- Good Christians do not fight.
- Collaboration is only possible when conflict is acknowledged, confronted, and dealt with.

Table 8.1 *(cont.)*	• The best way to deal with conflict is to ignore it. • Constructively dealing with conflict provides a sense of potency to the individuals involved. • Conflict not dealt with leads to individual pain and death to any collaborative effort. • Conflict produces tension.

Preparing for Conflict

Every conflict involves people who bring different personal backgrounds and personal histories to the situation. Each person has been raised and formed in a unique family situation within a particular culture and subculture, and these factors influence his or her needs, expectations, attitudes, convictions, and behaviors. In addition, two people in conflict sometimes bring a history to the situation. Therefore, approaching conflict requires considering the personalities involved, the specific situation, and the history of the relationship. Given that diversity, the suggestions covered in this section can provide a general framework for dealing more effectively with conflict.

Conflict would be more manageable if we knew in advance when and how it would occur. In reality, conflict usually emerges when it is least expected and often in ways never dreamed of. Since conflict generally takes people by surprise, those brilliant dialogues and rebuttals which most people have rehearsed in the privacy of their thoughts usually prove useless. When conflict erupts, the person's automatic response is to preserve his or her sense of self-esteem. This triggers a defensive reaction which interferes with the ability to listen clearly, think logically, and act compassionately, all of which are prerequisites for effective conflict management. Instead, with the onset of conflict, an unconscious or preconscious alarm system is tripped which sends out a single message: Protect yourself! The usual tendency is to defend by immediately attacking the other person. The more threatening the initial attack, the more intense the reaction against it. The conflict can escalate to the point where a rational solution is very difficult.

Conflict that can be anticipated is somewhat easier to deal with. Calling to mind a few basic principles can help in developing a more productive approach to the impending conflict.

1. Spend time clarifying the beliefs and attitudes which make you vulnerable to an attack.
2. Think about the needs, desires, and wants of the other person (group) which might precipitate or escalate the conflict.
3. Consider the practical factors—timing, communication, knowledge of the agenda—which could negatively or positively affect the situation.
4. If possible, find someone with whom to talk in order to gain greater insight into yourself and your strategies for dealing with the potential conflict.

Ask yourself questions, like those listed below, to help clarify your beliefs or attitudes about the conflict.

1. What is my greatest fear about this potential conflict?
2. What is the worst thing that could happen if conflict were to occur?
3. Why am I feeling so intense about this? What are my needs in this situation?
4. What history about myself or this relationship is unduly influencing me?
5. What might be encouraging me to avoid or escalate this conflict?
6. What will be my first reaction when the conflict occurs?
7. How are past experiences with this person (these people) influencing me?
8. Have I stored up unfinished business that is confusing the present issue?
9. How does my stereotyping of others influence my perception of the conflict and the possible outcome?

Although the answers to some of these questions reside in the unconscious, discussing them with someone who will do more than merely sympathize with you can be helpful. The person ought to know you well enough to challenge you regarding your planned responses and the corresponding actions.

After reflecting on yourself and your reactions, consider the other person who may be involved in the conflict:

1. What do you know about the other person that might help you to understand them better and to react more compassionately?
2. What do you know of the recent past of the other person which might influence their reaction?
3. What do you see as the strengths and good points of the other person?
4. Do you believe that all people are basically good?

Again, it is important to go through this process with someone who will challenge your perceptions and prevent you from stereotyping other people. The goal is not to label others but to become more free in responding with compassion, understanding, and rationality.

Dealing With Conflict

Although preparation for conflict is important, it does not guarantee successful resolution. The following suggestions are offered for dealing with conflict once it emerges:

1. Acknowledge the presence of the conflict.
2. Define the cause.
3. Make decisions.
4. Defuse the emotion.

Acknowledge the Presence of the Conflict

The spontaneous reaction to conflict for many ministers is denial. However, attempting to avoid the existence of the conflict usually leads to its escalation.

We were invited to work with a parish which the staff perceived as "the perfect parish." The "perfection" was achieved by eliminating anyone who might potentially cause conflict, especially those who were most traditional or most progressive. During our days with them, the disenchanted members of the congregation became more vocal. In representing their discontent to the parish staff, we experienced a hostile apathy, probably similar to what the confrontational members of the parish had received. It became evident that the primary goal of this staff was to ignore the presence of conflict. Since the ideas of the majority were never challenged, the parish continued to become more narrow in its perspective, less creative, and less life-giving. Only when conflict is acknowledged can it lead to growth for the individuals or group involved.

Define the Cause of the Conflict

Energy can be needlessly expended in dealing with the wrong issue. No resolution of conflict will occur until the real cause of the conflict has been identified and the energy has been directed toward it.

The most frequent causes of conflict are:

- threat to a basic need;
- poor communication;
- unfinished, unconscious personal development issues;
- loss.

These causes are explained in more detail as follows.

Threat to Needs

We believe that the most common cause of conflict is threat to a need. Since most behavior is need-directed, discovering the cause of conflict begins by identifying the needs which may be threatened. We will go one step further and suggest that the most frequent cause of conflict is the need to maintain a sense of self-esteem. Conflict usually occurs when more than one person's self-esteem is being threatened. When the participants are able to dispassionately discuss the feelings they experienced during the conflict, they almost invariably say that in some way they felt their value as a person was threatened.

There is a direct relationship between self-esteem and hostility. When self-esteem is low, hostility is high, and vice versa. One person feels his or her self-esteem is threatened and reacts by attacking others. The persons attacked experience a threat to *their* sense of well-being and counterattack in order to bolster their own self-esteem. The energy of everyone involved is absorbed in behavior directed toward maintaining self-esteem. Interestingly, a sense of lowered self-esteem is rarely expressed directly but is frequently manifested in indirect ways.

The issue over which people are in conflict is generally only symbolic of a deeper issue which is unconscious and/or too threatening to express directly. This is especially true whenever an inordinate amount of energy is expended in conflict over inanimate objects. Notice the intensity of emotion which can be generated at meetings over such issues as statues, keys, cars, altar railings, song books, and especially the liturgy. An outsider attending one of these emotionally charged discussions would have difficulty understanding how mature people could become so distraught over seemingly insignificant issues. Since arguing over object-related issues is less threatening than the personal issues which they represent, group leaders must learn to think symbolically. When a leader can look past the intense emotion focused on some inanimate object and determine what it symbolically represents, the real issue is often related to self-esteem.

Personality differences, which are commonly labeled as the source of conflict, are rarely if ever its real cause. People are capable of working well with many differing personalities, and differences only become an issue when one person's self-esteem is threatened by the other.

Likewise, power is usually only a secondary issue with the primary one being self-esteem or loss. Power becomes an issue when people feel impotent. In such a situation, a leader can be most helpful by not directing a response to the issue of power but by assisting the persons in conflict to clarify for themselves the feeling of helplessness and its effect on self-esteem and behavior.

Poor Communication

Conflicts which stem from poor communication can be readily addressed and easily resolved. Unfortunately, any institutional system can be fertile soil for breeding rumors. For the person attempting to mediate conflict, it is good to ascertain the information base from which people are working: What have they heard? Where have they heard it? How accurate is the information?

Developmental Issues

Still another cause of conflict might be described as unfinished personal development issues. No one has completely resolved all the residual conflicts from early childhood. Since the normal developmental tasks are not completed, each person unconsciously brings to new situations and relationships some of that unfinished conflict. One way people attempt to resolve the issues is by unconsciously projecting others into adversary roles with the hope that the previous conflict will be worked through in a more satisfactory way in the present.

An awareness of this dynamic, which is called *transference*, can help leaders understand some of the more confusing aspects of conflict. By transference an individual projects onto others qualities and reactions that are more appropriate to people from his or her earlier life and treats persons in the present as though they were those significant others from childhood. Two important aspects of transference are: the response is usually more intense than seems called for by the present situation; and the present reaction is asexual, that is, it may be to a male, even though the original reaction was to a female. While transference can be positive or negative, we refer here to negative transference which causes conflict. Since transference is an unconscious phenomenon, a person's resistance to admitting it may be very strong. Outside of a therapy situation, transference is best dealt with in an indirect way that helps the person see others as they really are, not as the person needs to see them.

Loss

A final cause of conflict, loss, is often manifested symbolically. Loss is a common cause of conflict, especially in parishes. In the last couple of decades, many have experienced significant losses within the church. Where personal identity was intrinsically entwined with identity as a Catholic—particularly pre-Vatican II Catholicism—the loss has been intense. These persons may feel that they have not only lost the religion which had profound meaning for them, but also have experienced a loss of part of themselves.

Loss usually produces great pain and anger. The anger can be suppressed, but it may seep out in conflicts over real but also symbolic losses in the present. This can explain the intense conflicts which emerge over such seemingly trivial losses as the removal of a statue. Too often ministers attempt to address this problem of loss by offering explanations; however, the pain is not felt in the mind but in the emotions. It is a heartache, not a headache. If a leader realizes that the conflict is an expression of the grieving process and responds not to the object of conflict but to the emotional level of pain, then the conflict can be managed or resolved.

Make Decisions About the Conflict

Once the real cause of the conflict has been isolated, the next step is to decide whether it is necessary to address the conflict and, if so, how to go about it. Ideally those involved in the conflict should reflect on a series of questions, like those below, which can help produce clarity regarding the decisions and can help prepare for the next steps of dealing with conflict:

- Do we believe that the time and energy expended in working through the conflict are justified? (Some issues are so insignificant that they do not warrant the time that must be diverted from ministry to deal with them.)
- How can we create a climate to most effectively deal with the conflict? (Again, when people feel safe there is a greater willingness to engage in conflict.)
- Do we have the skills to work through the conflict? (If not, the group should consider using the services of an outside facilitator.)
- What have we learned from past conflicts that can help with this one?

Defuse the Emotional Level

Defusing the emotional level of conflict is the responsibility of all involved. At times of conflict group members can become overly dependent on the designated leader and can avoid taking personal responsibility for improving the situation. One of the major tasks at these times is to defuse the emotional intensity of the situation to a level where people can interact rationally. When emotion is intense, most people experience anxiety which clouds perception and limits freedom to respond in a constructive way. In fact, unless there is a reduction in the level of emotional intensity (not the complete removal of it), the conflict will continue to be fanned into conflagration that, like fire, has the potential to destroy everything in its path.

The first step is contrary to the natural fight/flight reaction to conflict and consists in remaining in the situation and attempting to become as emotionally detached as possible. While we realize this is extremely difficult to accomplish, we are convinced that it is absolutely essential in helping a group deal effectively with the conflict.

Like any skill, emotional detachment is not easily or immediately learned and is acquired only after many attempts and failures. Proficiency in this skill requires trial and error; those who quit after a single unsuccessful attempt will never acquire the skill.

Once some relative detachment has been achieved, the next step is to help others do the same. The goal is to move people from the heart where the emotion is felt, to the head where some clarity emerges, to the mouth where the people involved are able to dialogue. They need to discover they are allies, not adversaries. Obtaining emotional distance from the conflict can be accomplished by taking some time away from the meeting and suggesting a few questions for reflection and prayer. The questions should challenge the participants to think about themselves, the cause of the conflict, and some of the reasons for the intensity of their feelings. Since conflict usually causes discomfort and pain, most people want to resolve the conflict. Providing time and distance will be appreciated, and it will usually be used to advantage. When the group reassembles, it is important to create a climate that facilitates the discussion.

At times of conflict leaders must assume a more directive approach. There are several things which can be done to help the group through this difficult process.

First, work at doing the unexpected. Since people generally expect others in a conflict situation to respond with elevated emotion, a response which is soft, unemotional, and compassionate has a disarming effect. Compassion is the antidote for hostility and can frequently transform the climate and elicit compassionate responses from others.

While conflict emphasizes the differences that exist between people, the leader can help the group members discover what they hold in common. Individual differences are more acceptable and can be productive when the group members realize they share a common goal or belief. People are not always aware of their commonality, and once the areas of commonality are made explicit, the probability of the conflict leading to growth is greatly enhanced.

During conflict the leader needs to draw upon the arsenal of leadership resources and skills that have been described earlier. The leader can:

- foster a climate where people feel heard and understood;
- challenge people to listen to each other;
- attempt to clear up ambiguity;
- clarify the real issue and keep the energy focused on that issue;
- continually summarize to maintain clarity;
- explore the "why" behind the "what."

Although beginning counseling courses discourage asking "why" questions, we have discovered that most conflict focuses on an issue without any understanding of why that issue has meaning to the persons involved. When the whys are explored there is often greater understanding, acceptance, and empathy.

Attempting Reconciliation

What happens after the conflict is just as important, if not more so, than the preparation or actual dealing with the conflict. As a Christian community we should not be surprised to find conflict, and we should be ready to challenge conflict when there is no attempt at reconciliation.

Our recommendation is to attempt reconciliation, realizing it cannot be forced. Unfortunately, there are people who do not want to be reconciled and who prefer, for whatever reasons, to nurture their hurts.

Many programs developed for priest support groups and for parish renewals emphasize reconciliation. It is the element of reconciliation which often provides the climate for real sharing and growth. Whenever there has been a rupture of relationships through conflict, we strongly recommend that there be some attempt at reconciliation. It is not the presence of conflict which impedes the continued growth toward collaboration, but the lack of forgiveness and reconciliation.

Years of working with collaborative groups has convinced us that a Christian community is not characterized by the absence of conflict, but it should be distinguished by the presence of forgiveness and attempts at reconciliation. (More on the topic of forgiveness appears in two previous works, *Design for Wholeness* and *Building Community*.) The USCCB has recently published a document on forgiveness reminding that forgiveness is a modeling of God in the community:

> We must acknowledge the profound truth that reconciliation is not simply an end in itself; reconciliation is for the sake of communion—communion with the Triune God and communion with each other. There can be no forgiveness and reconciliation without unity and communion with God and with one another (J2, p. 13).

Table 8.2

A Summary of Stages of Conflict
I. Prepare for the Conflict
    A. Clarify beliefs
    B. Think about the other person
    C. Consider practical factors
    D. Seek consultation
II. Deal with the Conflict
    A. Acknowledge the conflict
    B. Define the cause
        1. needs
        2. communication
        3. developmental issues
        4. loss
    C. Make decisions about the conflict
    D. Defuse the emotional level
III. Attempt Reconciliation

Conclusion

Conflict is stressful and frequently painful. Healthy people detest conflict. However, failure to deal with conflict is a sure death knell for any collaborative effort. Many ministers, both ordained and non-ordained, admit their inadequacies in dealing with conflict. Initial and continuing formation programs for ministers should include skill development in conflict resolution and management.

Reflection/Discussion Questions

1. What are some of my beliefs about conflict which influence how I deal with conflict?
2. Where have I acquired the skills for dealing with conflict? How will I develop additional skills in this area?
3. How does our group deal with conflict? Is this method for dealing with it constructive or destructive? What are some additional ways to deal with conflict?

9

Confrontation

When people are asked what image they associate with confrontation, the responses are often described in negative, violent, or destructive terms. Given these images, it is no wonder that confrontation is avoided whenever possible. There is a general inability for individuals to identify times when confrontation could be labeled successful. The general reluctance to attempt confrontation can stem from fears or negative attitudes, lack of skills, or previous negative experiences. Like conflict, it is not confrontation which hinders collaboration. It is the unwillingness or inability of ministers to engage in confrontation when necessary which interferes with the development of greater collaboration.

One way to increase competency is to consider confrontation from the following perspectives: what, why, who, when, and how.

Confrontation Defined

What is confrontation? A dictionary definition of confrontation is "to cause to meet" or "to bring face to face." Though generally associated with opposition, confrontation does not necessarily imply that people face each other as adversaries; they can come together in friendship too. For our purposes, to confront means to bring people face-to-face to look at the same situation.

To further expand, confrontation can also mean to place the truth, as one person sees it, in front of another. Since each person views life through a limited perspective, confrontation implies that no one has all the truth but only one aspect of it.

An expanded notion of confrontation reduces the anxiety connected with it and affects why and how a person approaches confrontation.

Reasons for Confrontation

"Why" is an important question and is usually the key determining factor in the success of confrontation. One reason for confrontation is to search for a more complete picture of the truth. In essence the person is saying, "Let me tell you how I see the situation. I realize that my perspective is limited, and I want to know how you see it so that together we can come to a fuller appreciation of the truth." The goal of confrontation is to search for the truth which is not the exclusive domain of any one individual. Rather, pieces of the truth exist in many different individuals. Confrontation allows for a more thorough search for the whole truth.

Confrontation generally accomplishes positive results when it is motivated by care and concern for the well-being of the other. A few years ago a member of a parish team indicated that she had experienced severe depression and burnout. She shared how different members of the staff had confronted her about her behavior. The woman could only listen to those who communicated their concern for her; she "turned off" other staff members.

A pre-arranged agreement for mutual accountability can be another reason for confrontation. For instance, if a staff has agreed upon certain expectations, the members have a right to confront each other when someone fails to behave in ways consistent with those agreed-upon expectations.

Confrontation fails when the unspoken message is, "I'm telling you this because what you do annoys me, and I expect you to change." Usually the one confronting merely becomes frustrated because the desired results are not forthcoming. Frustration produces anger which, in turn, will probably be communicated to the other person and be experienced as hostility. This is far from the goal of confrontation, which is to foster dialogue.

Confrontation is most successful when there is a reciprocal search for truth; it is motivated by care and concern; or there has been an agreement about mutual accountability.

People Involved in Confrontation

When a person confronts another he or she should do so out of care for the person. When this concern is conveyed, a climate is created where the individuals can dialogue.

In some instances, confrontation is delegated to a certain person because of his or her role. When a confrontation occurs because of role rather than concern, no positive results should be expected. In fact, when those in authority convey the impression that they are confronting only because it is expected in their position or role, the reaction is usually resistance or hostility.

When Confrontation Is Warranted

Although no time is perfect, choosing an occasion with the greatest possibility of listening and openness on both sides is desirable. For example, confronting people who are physically or emotionally too exhausted to listen or share is counterproductive. Under such conditions, confrontations can easily deteriorate into emotional, hostile, shouting matches. Before initiating confrontation, assess the climate and surrounding conditions.

Both parties need time to internalize what is said and to engage in whatever dialogue is necessary to reach understanding. The "Do-you-have-two-minutes-there-is-something-I-want-to-tell-you" approach is generally doomed to failure. Absence of a sense of control often moves a confrontation into a conflict. Informing the person that you would like to discuss an issue that will probably take "x" minutes, and setting a time to meet, gives the other person some control.

Since the automatic response to a critical confrontation is defensiveness, it is advisable to tell the person what issue you want to discuss. This allows the other person time and distance to develop a response. When the dialogue immediately follows the confrontation, the goal is often self-protection rather than understanding. The initiator of a confrontation has had time to prepare, but the other person may be taken by surprise. Offering that person the opportunity to reflect, pray, or talk with another before responding to what has been shared often creates a climate for mutual understanding and dialogue.

Finally, people operate on different time clocks. One person may want to resolve all issues immediately, another may need a longer time in order to dialogue rationally. This aspect has to be considered and discussed among the parties involved.

Ways to Confront Another

The skills involved in the "how" aspect of confrontation are the most critical of the five perspectives. The seven principles which follow are guidelines for developing skill in confrontation. Some of the skills needed for confrontation are the same as those described in detail in the previous chapter.

1. When possible, confront in the first person. Phrases such as, "I heard that . . . " or "They said . . . " imply a "marshalling of the troops" and elicit a self-protective and defensive response from the person being confronted. Confrontations are usually more effective when the person doing the confronting speaks about what he or she has observed.

2. Do not confront on behalf of others. An individual who confronts because of care and concern for the other person will be better received than an individual who confronts because he or she has been delegated by others. Sometimes a leader is asked to confront an individual on behalf of others. If a leader does not share the group's concern, he or she can be most helpful by encouraging them to do the confronting themselves. The leader should work with the group to clarify the reasons and goals for the confrontation. Reviewing some general principles for confrontation is also useful.

3. Be direct and gentle. As already mentioned in Chapter 7, combining directness with gentleness usually produces positive results. People who are very direct and honest, but lack gentleness or compassion, are often surprised when those they confront react defensively, aggressively, or hostilely. Likewise, when fear of confrontation causes the one confronting to be excessively vague in expressing his or her reasons for concern, the other person may leave confused, without even realizing that he or she has just been confronted. Being direct and gentle generally produces the best results. However, confrontation, like conflict, is never easy, and following this and other recommendations will not assure success. Learning to combine gentleness with directness is like engaging in a complex dance. It takes great skill, a skill which is often acquired only after a series of "failures." Most people are better at one or the other dimension. They are either direct or gentle. Integrating the two is the secret for success in confrontation.

4. Keep confrontation in the present. A confrontation can easily move beyond present behavior to a litany of past behaviors. This kind of bombardment makes it impossible for the person to listen. When this occurs the purpose of the confrontation is undermined. When comments are limited to what has been observed most recently, the potential for being heard and understood is augmented.

5.Confront the behavior, not the person. Distinguishing between the person and the behavior is not easy, and we merely suggest that working to develop this discriminating posture is a good principle. However, there is no assurance that the person being confronted will be able to make the same distinction.

6. Never interpret behavior. Confrontations can readily erupt into irreconcilable conflicts when the ones confronting go beyond describing what they have observed, and ascribe intentions to the behavior. "You did thus and so because. . . ." No one can interpret the causes of another's behavior based solely on observation. Any given behavior can have multiple causes. For example, a person's roommates may not have washed the dishes as they had agreed to do because: they forgot, they were being hostile, they were called out on emergency, they are immature and irresponsible, they have an aversion to order, they see messy dishes as "homey," and so on. Any or none of these reasons could explain the roommates' behavior.

The fact is that the motivation for behavior rests with the person, not in an outsider's interpretation of it. Normally, if one interprets another person's behavior, it is in the light of his or her own personal experiences, history, and beliefs. A person's experiences help to form beliefs. Beliefs produce feelings and needs which, in turn, are often expressed as behavior. The flow chart summarizes:

EXPERIENCE — BELIEFS — FEELINGS — BEHAVIOR

An observer sees only the outcome of the process, not the steps leading up to it. For instance, suppose that whenever Mr. Z talks at a staff meeting, no one responds. Mr. Z may assume that everyone thinks what he says is stupid or of little importance. Actually, it may be that Mr. Z's comments are so profound that everyone else becomes reflective. However, Mr. Z may begin to feel stupid; his self-esteem is lowered. As a result he becomes very withdrawn and stops contributing at meetings. The only thing that the others see is his now silent behavior, and all sorts of incorrect interpretations could be ascribed to it.

Confrontation should be limited to observed behavior, the only area where there is any certainty, and no attempt should be made to analyze the causes of the behavior.

7. Be willing to listen and to be confronted by those whom you confront. This is perhaps the most frightening part of confrontation, as well as the most important. Beginning from the premise that each person has only a part of the truth and that one of the goals in confrontation is to come to a fuller appreciation of the truth, it is essential that the other be encouraged to share how the situation looks from his or her perspective. In the above example, suppose Mrs. Q became concerned about Mr. Z's silence and decided to confront him about it. Hopefully Mrs. Q would listen to Mr. Z describe the situation as he experienced it, and together they could dialogue in order to develop a fuller picture. Confrontation is most productive when all the parties involved are willing to be confronted with new pieces of the truth.

As a final point, there are times after confrontation has occurred when someone in authority has to intervene. For example, if an alcoholic person has been confronted about his or her self-destructive behavior and has not changed, then in charity and justice a person in authority may have to inform the alcoholic that a decision has been made, for example, that he or she will go to a treatment center. However, a decision should be imposed only after confrontation has been tried.

Table 9.1

Summary of Principles of Confrontation
A. What is confrontation?
   1. A bringing of individuals face-to-face to look at the same situation.
   2. Articulating the truth, as seen by one individual, to another.
B. Why confront?
   1. To encourage dialogue in a search for the truth.
   2. Because there is a genuine concern for the other.
   3. There has been a specific agreement about mutual accountability.
C. Who should confront?
   1. The person who is perceived as one who truly cares about the other.
D. When to confront?
   1. When there is the greatest potential for a climate that the one confronted will be able to listen to, hear, and understand the one doing the confronting.
   2. When there is adequate time to prepare a response rather than a reaction.
   3. At a time that is conducive to both parties.

Table 9.1 (continued)	E. How to confront?

E. How to confront?
1. Always confront in the first person.
2. Select as the one doing the confronting the person most likely to be heard and listened to.
3. Be direct and gentle.
4. Restrict the incidents described to those which have occurred in the recent past.
5. Confront the behavior, not the person.
6. Do not interpret behavior.
7. Be open to be confronted in return.

Conclusion

Confrontation, like conflict, is a difficult skill to acquire. When mature adults are involved in collaborating, there is often the need to confront others for the sake of the mission. Passivity, in the face of the need for confrontation, is an obstacle to collaboration. The skill of confronting, like the skills of group leadership and dealing with conflict, should be an integral part of any ministry formation program.

Reflection/Discussion Questions

1. Recall a time when you engaged a confrontation. Using Table 9.1 (page 145), evaluate yourself. What do you learn about successful confrontation from your reflection on this experience? How would you do it differently?
2. Recall a time when you were confronted. Attempt to recapture and relive that experience. How did the attitude and actions of the other either facilitate or hinder your ability to accept what was being said?
3. What have you learned from past experiences with confrontation that can help you in the future?

10

Structure and Process for Collaborative Ministry

Thus far the discussion of collaborative ministry has encompassed the following:

- its evolution;
- myths and misconceptions about the concept;
- required skills and attitudes needed to be collaborative;
- a developmental readiness and a spirituality for collaborative ministry.

We now draw attention to the area that will move a group beyond the desire for greater collaboration toward the reality of it. If this is to happen, the implementation of collaborative ministry demands a process and adequate structures.

The process will vary according to the specific composition, history, and goals of the group. That being said, there are some key elements which must be part of any process if greater collaboration is to occur. We have identified four elements (see Table 10.1) that are integral to any process of collaboration. Though the phrasing differs, these elements complement the "practical steps" identified by the United States bishops in *From Words to Deeds: Continuing Reflections on the Role of Women in the Church*. The presence of these elements greatly enhances the probability for success. Their absence usually results in frustration and fragmentation.

	Our Key Elements	*Practical Steps* *"From Words to Deeds"*
Table 10.1	1. a vision with concrete objectives;	1. examine our beliefs and behaviors and confront those that hinder our ability to collaborate;
	2. a method for identifying the gifts of the community members;	2. discernment of gifts;
	3. clarity of roles;	3. clarify roles;
	4. empower a group to implement collaboration	4. develop the necessary skills;
		5. nurture the spiritual foundation on which collaboration rests.

Since spirituality and skills have been discussed in earlier chapters, the following pages will develop the remaining areas raised in these two models:

- examining one's attitudes and beliefs;
- developing a clear vision;
- discerning gifts;
- clarifying roles;
- empowering a group to implement collaboration.

Examining Attitudes and Beliefs

The Diocese of Albany has identified collaborative ministry as the major priority of the diocese. Bishop Howard Hubbard identified the following key beliefs about collaborative ministry:

- it is "based on the baptismal call";
- every member of the church has received this call;
- the call is given to "advance the mission and ministry of Jesus in our world."

In a talk to a national gathering of pastoral planners, Bishop Hubbard developed further a list of attitudes and beliefs about collaborative efforts in ministry. Use the list to help analyze your own attitudes and beliefs about collaboration.

⇨ The church exists to be in service to the world.

⇨ The church is a community of ministers responsible for "bringing the healing presence of Christ to a wounded humanity."

⇨ The major function of church leaders is to encourage and empower all the baptized to utilize their gifts in mission.

⇨ Leaders must develop "smaller units where a sense of community can be nurtured and fostered."

⇨ Effective collaborative ministry requires a commitment to details and must be "nurtured and implemented patiently and sensitively."

⇨ Collaborative skills must be developed.

⇨ Spirituality provides the basis for collaborative ministry.

⇨ Church leaders must witness a commitment to collaborative ministry by their actions, not just their rhetoric.

⇨ Church leaders must make a substantial financial commitment to supporting the laity in acquiring the education and formation needed to function effectively in collaboration.

⇨ The church must evaluate its programs and services to determine whether they really respond to the "felt needs within our parish communities" (NCP).

Compare your beliefs and attitudes with those listed above. What are the beliefs which influence your personal commitment to collaborative ministry? Do those beliefs facilitate or hinder your ability to collaborate more fully?

Developing a Vision

To paraphrase the Proverb 29:18, "Where there is no vision, the people perish."

Jesus had a clear vision of the mission for which he had come into the world. This vision, to bring all people to knowledge of and union with his Father, served as the criterion for all his activity. Like Jesus, all Christians—individuals and groups—must have a clear vision which guides all their actions and decisions.

Many good projects, whether at the diocesan, parish, or community level, flounder or fail due to the absence of an articulated vision which clearly defines the direction. It is vitally important that a vision be clear, mission-oriented, and mutually agreed upon by those who will be affected by it.

Table 10.2

Criteria for Developing a Vision
1. A vision gives a general direction. In order to be effective, visions need to be accompanied by specific goals.
2. A vision is expansive, rather than restrictive.
3. A vision must be owned by those who are affected by it.
4. An effective vision moves to action as a result of concrete implementation steps.

Visions can be meaningless, self-aggrandizing statements unless accompanied by clear goals for implementation. The presence of explicitly stated goals can serve to offset frustration which can arise from directionless activity.

There are groups that articulate an extremely narrow vision while restricting collaboration among a small number of people, such as a staff. When a group's vision is too narrowly focused, a relatively high degree of ennui, disappointment, and apathy can result. A Christian community is called to move beyond a vision of mere intra-community concern to one which aspires to greater collaboration with the wider community. The USCCB, reflecting on the call of every Christian to community, cautions against a community which is excessively self-absorbed:

> Members of such communities should be as ready for engagement with the world outside their community as they are for deepening their relationship within it (CG, p. 13).

A diocese or parish, for instance, needs to think beyond collaboration among its staff members and ask the more important question: How do we find additional ways to utilize the gifts of all the baptized who have been gifted and called for ministry? Vision statements are most life-giving when they are mission-oriented and offer a challenge to incorporate and to influence beyond the immediate group.

Besides setting a vision, an additional dimension must be considered: Whose vision is it? Only persons who have the opportunity to participate in the formulation of the vision will be committed to it. Individuals or elite groups who frame a vision and then expect commitment from those who were excluded from the direction-setting process should not be surprised when they experience resistance and rejection. If the goal is collaboration, then the ideal is to involve everyone who is potentially affected.

Although this is an obvious principle, many examples to the contrary can be cited:

- the diocese which develops and disseminates a mission statement formulated by a small group of diocesan staff or a pastoral council;
- a staff which promulgates a parish vision statement developed exclusively by the staff;
- the religious congregation that designs mission plans for apostolates and corporate works without consulting those who will be affected;
- the leader who functions in isolation and then proclaims a vision for the group.

Where there is no vision the people perish. Where the people affected by the vision are not involved in formulating it, the predicted outcome is apathy.

In order for an articulated, mutually-owned vision to bear fruit there must be an explicit, concrete commitment to implement that vision. If a group has developed a vision to which it is truly committed, that vision will begin to influence all decisions about priorities, programs, budget, and time. Vision statements that are articulated in the comfort and serenity of a quiet weekend at some isolated location can soon be forgotten as daily demands are placed upon the ministers when they return to their normal setting. The challenge of a vision statement is to bring it to fruition regardless of the effort that is demanded and the difficulties encountered.

Many groups who have struggled to formulate a clear vision statement have devised creative ways of communicating it, and yet have experienced discouragement because no growth has resulted. Unless the direction provided by the vision is accompanied by concrete steps to achieve it, little change will occur.

The importance of developing specific plans to achieve a goal was clearly illustrated in a parish where the pastoral minister, a religious brother, was informed by his community that his ministry to the sick and homebound of the parish was limited to a three-year commitment. The community also informed the parish that they had no one to send as a replacement after the three years. The parish staff recognized and articulated the need to identify lay leadership to continue this valuable and necessary ministry. At the end of the first year it was apparent to the staff that nothing had occurred to bring the parish closer to this goal. Specific objectives were then defined to move the vision toward reality. The immediate goal was to identify ten parishioners who possessed the gifts to minister to the sick. During his second year, the brother would spend half of his time training these new ministers. The goal for the end of the second year was to identify at least two people who had the leadership qualities to run the program and to see that, during the brother's final year, these individuals received the training necessary to direct the program.

Table 10.3	*Vision Statement*
	Visions will bear fruit when:
	• there are goals to accompany the vision;
	• the vision is more externally focused than narrowly defined;
	• everyone affected by the vision has been included in the process of developing it; and,
	• concrete methods for implementing the vision have been developed.

Examine your group's vision statement. Which, if any, of these above criteria are part of your process?

Discerning Gifts

The essence of collaborative ministry is identifying, releasing, and uniting all the gifts present in the community for the sake of mission. Therefore, any process to facilitate collaborative ministry must include, as a core element, a method for identifying gifts. Collaboration based on anything other than gifts is artificial and doomed to failure. This is a conviction we have held since first writing on collaborative ministry (1987). Numerous experiences over the years have only served to confirm this conviction. *From Words to Deeds* likewise emphasizes the need for discernment of gifts:

> A second practical step involves discernment of gifts. In a collaborative effort, individual gifts must be affirmed by the group. Some groups use a discernment process that identifies the obvious and not-so-obvious gifts of the individual. The process can help individuals—clergy, religious, laity—to recognize and value gifts and talents that they have overlooked or considered commonplace. It affirms the unique contribution that he or she makes to the common effort (FWD, p. 20).

As mentioned in Chapter 1, collaboration is the union of *all* the gifts in the community. The USCCB document *Called and Gifted for the Third Millennium* stresses the fact that gift and call must be viewed as two parts of the same reality. Cardinal Mahony describes this union further:

> The Spirit of God has provided gifts to all . . . for the good of the Church. . . . The priestly ministry of Jesus is not fully exercised if these gifts of the Spirit are not exercised for the community and mission of the Church. . . . Each of us is a poor steward of our gifts if we do not see them as gifts to be given . . . for the sake of the human community (PAL, p. 19f).

Mahony also reminds us that the gifts are to be used not only "within the formal Church structures" but "to family, work, and world." Or as *From Words to Deeds* puts it:

All the faithful are challenged to use their gifts to further Christ's mission in the world. All must participate to build the reign of God (FWD, p. 19).

As noted earlier, *From Words to Deeds* calls for pastors, and by extension, all church leaders to bring forth the gifts of all, and to work to overcome whatever obstacles prevent those gifts from being put at the service of ministry and mission. Listed as a practical step in Table 10.1 is the invitation and challenge to engage in a process of mutual discernment of gifts. One of the fruits of identifying and uniting gifts is that it brings life to the parish and to other church organizations. The sociological research by Castelli and Gremillion confirm this. Their research indicates that pastors cite involvement of the laity as the top reason for parish vitality.

For almost twenty years we have been working with groups striving to achieve greater collaboration. During that time, nothing has been more satisfying and effective than engaging groups in a process of identifying and releasing gifts. Group after group reported that the gift discernment process energized them and helped them direct their collaborative efforts in a more organized and life-giving way.

There are various ways to identify the gifts of the community. Among the models which have been used successfully by ministry groups certain common elements emerge, for example:

- creating a climate in which people feel free to discern their gifts;
- developing a method for sharing and clarifying the individual gifts;
- examining ways these gifts can be used in ministry.

Certain conditions are necessary to create a climate in which people feel free to discern their gifts. First, adequate time must be allowed for private, prayerful reflection on one's own gifts and the gifts of others in the group. Any of the scriptural passages which refer to gifts may be helpful, e.g., Romans 12:8 or 1 Corinthians 12:4-11, 12-26. Second, physical surroundings should be conducive to dialogue. Third, the participants should know one another well. When this third factor is absent, the entire process may be experienced as a game or a playful technique. Finally, an objective presentation can help set the tone and direction for the gift discernment. Such a presentation could discuss personal obstacles which make it difficult to identify gifts, aspects of giftedness, and some examples of the meaning of giftedness.

The gift discernment models which produce the most desirable results are those in which each person shares the personal gifts he or she has identified. The others respond to the speaker by affirming and naming additional gifts they feel the person possesses. It is important to keep in mind that many ministers overemphasize their gifts of *doing* to the exclusion of their gifts of *being*. A balance of the two aspects is ideal.

While gift discernment is usually a very affirming experience for those who participate, affirmation is not the primary purpose. The goal is to discern a person's call to ministry based on his or her gifts and to determine how those gifts can be combined with others for effective ministry. When conducting gift discernment processes such as the one described in *Building Community* (pp. 67-75), we end the process by inviting those who have participated to reflect on a series of issues and questions like those that follow:

- Gift and call always exist together. If these are your gifts, how and where are you being called to use them?
- Each one is responsible for the development of the gift God has given. What do you need to do to develop your gifts?
- There is a responsibility to assist other community members in releasing their gifts in service and in ministry. What do you need from your community to release and maximize your gifts?
- The union of gifts is the quintessence of collaborative ministry. How can your gifts be connected with others' gifts to more effectively foster the mission of Jesus?

Ideally, after the initial gift discerning experience, the participants gather again to choose an area of ministry based on their gifts and the perceived needs of their particular situation. They then explore together ways in which their individual gifts can unite in ministry.

One aspect of gift discernment that seems particularly relevant in our culture today is the challenge to value the diversity of gifts. Maria Harris in her exemplary book, *Proclaim Jubilee! A Spirituality for the Twenty-First Century*, relates a poignant story of the value of and need for an appreciation of this diversity:

> When the world Council of Churches met in Sydney, Australia more than a decade ago, Krister Stendahl, then dean of Harvard Divinity School, noted that whenever an issue was brought to the table, it got four characteristic responses: Latin Americans responded with customary passion; Africans asked what the implications were for the community; Asians reflected quietly in contemplative mindfulness; and North Americans inquired, "What are we going to do?" The point of this recollection is not to set these responses in conflict. Instead, it is to note that we need all four perspectives. We need passion *and* community *and* contemplative being *and* active intervention when responding to suffering.

Clarifying Roles

The delineation of roles can be an area of ambiguity which could lead to tension and conflict. The gift discernment process promotes the clarification of roles and achieves a greater clarity in the use of gifts.

> . . . This identification of gifts helps to clarify roles. Clarity about roles and responsibilities helps to avoid the "turf wars" that threaten collaboration. Convinced that their gifts are recognized and valued, people are more likely to focus on doing their own tasks well in order to achieve the group's mission (FWD, p. 20).

We suggest four avenues to consider in clarifying roles:

- the relationship between roles and gifts;
- the degree of exhaustion;
- the extent to which ministry is performed collaboratively;
- the continuation of ministries.

These avenues are explained further in the remainder of this section.

Relationship Between Roles and Gifts

Frequently roles are assigned on the basis of a particular state in life or a specific sex, for example, "Father (*because he is a priest*) will lead the prayers" or "Mrs. X (*because she is a woman*) will take the minutes." On the other hand, there may be such a reaction to this stereotyping that Father is *never* asked to lead the prayers or Mrs. X is *never* asked to serve as secretary even though she has the gifts. Neither role nor sex should be the criterion upon which ministries are chosen. The appropriate question asks: Who has the gifts to best perform this particular ministry?

Ministers are most effective when the role required of them is compatible with their natural and acquired gifts, talents, and skills. While this may seem like an obvious statement, it is not always the criterion upon which ministries are assigned or chosen. Too frequently specific ministries are determined by tradition, random selection, or rotation. A planning process which helps identify specific areas of ministerial need and assists individuals to select ministry based on their gifts and talents is far more desirable.

What we are describing is an ideal. We realize that some church structures deny certain roles on the basis of sex or vocational choice. This is a problem, but it is also a reality. While we empathize with those who feel anger as a result of this situation, we also caution against converting that anger into hostility which destroys further collaboration. We encourage seeking positive ways to express the anger and frustration.

Degree of Exhaustion

In group training programs we ask leaders in training to assess their level of tiredness after conducting a group session. A high level of physical and emotional exhaustion can indicate that the leader is assuming inordinate responsibility for the group, thereby minimizing the potential of the group. Ministers can easily succumb to this same tendency.

The desire to serve and to participate in the church's mission can become overshadowed by the human need for affirmation and self-esteem. Assuming sole and complete responsibility for a project not only unnecessarily drains a person's physical and emotional energy but also deprives others of the opportunity to bring their talents to a particular project.

An incident on a college campus exemplifies this attitude. While the students and faculty members looked on, the campus minister prepared the altar for the celebration, served as lector, led the singing, and then distributed communion. Her behavior seemed in opposition to the college's goal of forming Christian leaders. We could not help but wonder to what extent her own needs were being met inordinately through her ministry.

Ministers who excel at doing for others often find it difficult to be on the receiving end of ministry. These are the people who are always complaining of being exhausted. They are only comfortable in the role of giver, and cannot allow others in the community to use their gifts in ministering to them.

Recently we visited a member of a religious community just before his death. He began crying and described how difficult it was for him to be on the receiving end of ministry. He articulated that it was easier and more comfortable to be the dispenser of ministry rather than being the recipient of it. His experience is not an unusual one. He was capable of honestly admitting the reality, but too many people involved in ministry are unable to acknowledge their need to be in the role of giver and dispenser of ministry.

Ministering Collaboratively

A major role for anyone in ministry is helping individuals in the Christian community respond to their call to ministry. The transition from the traditional role of minister as doer to minister as enabler is not an easy one and may trigger feelings of ambivalence. The desire to move toward collaboration is often coupled with fear. Unless there is willingness on the part of ministers to acknowledge ambivalence and to identify the causes of resistance, any attempts at collaboration will probably be prematurely aborted.

Ministers who believe that everyone is called and gifted recognize the gifts of others and challenge them to join in some form of mutual ministry. One way to measure our disposition toward enablement is by examining our ministry experiences. Are there aspects of ministry in which we could involve others? The chart in Table 10. 4 deals with specific situations, but it can be used as a model for describing our present ministries and our attitude toward enabling others.

Table 10.4

Process for Evaluating Progress as an Enabler

Individual	Advisory	Assistance	Collaborative	Enabling
"I do"	*"I do, they advise"*	*"I do, they help"*	*"We do"*	*"They do"*
I teach a religious class	I ask parents about the needs of the children	I have an assistant in the classroom	Co-teacher and I teach class, review material, and decide content	Co-teacher becomes teacher
I facilitate meetings of divorced people	I gather groups of divorced to help me prepare program	I have a divorced person assist me in the group	We co-lead group, share responsibilities equally	Divorced people run a ministry for one another
I visit the sick parishioners	I gather some people who reflect on the needs of the sick	I ask a parishioner to assist on a home visit	Parishioner and I visit sick and share reflections on the experience	Parish visitation ministry is administered by parishioners

Continuation of Ministries

It is often valuable to reflect on previous ministry situations. Ask yourself these questions:

- How many ministries in which you have been engaged have you passed on to others?
- When you left your last ministry placement, did the work continue without you?

- Had you worked with and formed others in the local community to take responsibility for the continuation of the ministry?

The ultimate criterion for evaluating ministry is often what continued after the minister left! A good measuring stick is anytime you do for others what they can do for themselves, you are probably not doing it for God or for the sake of the mission, but rather to meet your own needs.

Given that the number of members of religious congregations is decreasing, religious can no longer be assured that they will be replaced by members of their own community or other communities. One pastoral minister, a sister, shared with us that in the last two parishes she had included in her contract that she would not be replaced by another religious when she was transferred. In both cases she helped identify gifted people in the local community who could carry on her ministry and arranged for them to receive the necessary training.

Empowering a Group to Implement Collaborative Ministry

Many leaders already feel over-burdened and stretched beyond their limits. Stressed leaders are not able to accept any new responsibilities, and collaborative ministry may fall into this category. Ideally, a specific group could be empowered to foster the development of collaborative ministry. This group would develop its own model out of its unique circumstances. For example, a parish model that has proven successful is based on the parish pastoral council. This model, could be adapted for specific circumstances, and could be useful in other situations as well.

The most effective model for pastoral councils, we believe, is one developed by the Canadian Conference of Catholic Bishops. Their *Parish Pastoral Council* document states that the major purpose of the council is to develop the parish as "a living Christian community." They identify the three major tasks of such a council:

1. to identify needs;
2. to discern the gifts and resources available; and,
3. to establish the structures to bring about a marriage between the needs and gifts/resources.

Such an understanding of councils is truly collaborative. It identifies the areas in need of ministry, searches for the gifts which are present in the community to respond to those needs, and develops the structure to wed the needs and gifts.

The role of the pastoral council as it relates to collaborative ministry is also described in great clarity by Bishop Hubbard:

> The parish council . . . strives to give the members of the parish the ability to exercise their gifts and talents so that the parish itself is a truly vibrant expression of God's loving, healing, liberating and redemptive presence among us. The council is a practical means of achieving the full participation of the whole parish in its mission. . . . The parish becomes a community of collaborative ministry (GPP).

Conclusion

Collaborative ministry does not happen automatically or easily. It demands attention to both processes and structures. Among the processes which facilitate collaborative ministry are: the formulation of a clear, realistic, and shared vision; a mechanism for the identification and union of gifts; the articulation of beliefs; the clarification of roles; the development of the requisite skills; the deepening of a collaborative spirituality; and the empowerment of a group to implement the collaborative vision.

Reflection/Discussion Questions

The following questions are grouped among the four processes and structures of collaborative ministry.

Vision
1. How does our vision provide us with a sense of direction for planning and evaluation?
2. How have we included everyone who will be affected by the vision?
3. How does the vision explicitly challenge us to even broader collaboration?

4. How do we allow time to build the attitudes and skills necessary to accomplish the vision?
5. How much of the budget is allocated for collaborative efforts and development?
6. How committed are we to continuing to build greater collaboration in spite of the difficulties, conflicts, or pain encountered?

Identifying the Gifts
7. When and how do we discern gifts?
8. How much emphasis is placed on gifts of being rather than doing?
9. How is the gift discernment process used to determine ministries?

Clarity of Roles
10. To what extent are ministries assigned on the basis of perceived giftedness?
11. Who are the people I have challenged and enabled to become involved in ministry?
12. How would I like to change my approach to ministry?

Assessing Biases
13. Complete the following sentences. List the first thought that comes to mind. Be honest and avoid any immediate censuring.
    Most priests . . .
    Laity are . . .
    Deacons usually . . .
    Brothers never . . .
    Sisters always . . .
14. Is there anything in the attitudes revealed by your responses in question 13 which could make it difficult for you to work with some members of the Christian community? How were some of your responses influenced by painful past experiences? (Realizing that isolated incidents may be continuing to influence present perceptions is the first step in overcoming stereotypes which may interfere with collaboration.)

11

Collaborative Ministry in Practice

This final chapter looks at some examples of collaborative ministry in practice. As we have noted previously, the face of collaboration takes shape and form from each unique situation. We selected three projects as examples of successful collaborative endeavors, and interviewed a representative from each in order to obtain feedback on their collaborative experiences. There are many other projects, parishes, and dioceses in different geographical locations where collaboration is indeed alive and working. The three examples that we have selected simply represent a cross-section of successful collaborative projects. Collaboration is never completed. It is always in process and these three projects illustrate that fact. The three projects of focus are:

- an inter-congregational health care facility;
- a parish;
- an educational institution.

Each interviewee responded to the following questions:

- What motivated the people who began this program?
- Why are you convinced of the need for collaboration?
- What are the greatest obstacles encountered?
- From your experience what would you recommend to others?
- What have you learned about collaboration from this experience?

We will summarize and offer our observations on each interview. Finally, we share the findings from a research project conducted on collaboration in the not-for-profit sector.

Project 1: Inter-Community Health Care, Inc.

Interviewee:
Sister Marjorie Hebert, MSC, Executive Director
Address:
Our Lady of Wisdom Health Care Center
Inter-Community Health Care, Inc.
5600 General DeGaulle Drive
New Orleans, LA 90103
Phone:
504-394-5991
Fax:
504-304-5421
E-mail:
margemsc@msn.com

Background Information

The project was first proposed at a meeting of major superiors of congregations of religious men and women in New Orleans, Louisiana. There are sixteen congregations involved in the project representing almost 1,300 religious. The congregations represent a broad spectrum from cloistered to apostolic congregations. There are twelve women's congregations and four men's congregations.

This collaborative group has recently opened a 138-bed skilled-care facility capable of accepting Alzheimer's patients and equipped for rehabilitation services. There are future plans to develop a dementia daycare facility. A certain percentage of the beds have been approved for Medicare and Medicaid patients.

From the group of sixteen congregations, seven assumed the responsibilities of ownership and formed a corporation. Each of the corporate members has a representative on the board of directors. Representatives from the other nine congregations form a consultative group and meet with the board of directors at least two times a year. At some time in the future, members from this consultative group will fill positions on an expanded Board of Directors.

The financial contribution from each congregation is determined by ability to contribute. The contributions range from $250 to over one million dollars.

Motivation for Initiating the Project

The motivation was simple: there was a common need. No one congregation alone could afford to continue a long-termed skilled care for their aging, sick members in that geographic area.

Reasons for Being Convinced of the Value of Collaboration

There was a plethora of reasons for the need to be collaborative:

- Although some congregations were financially able to maintain their own facilities, at least for the time being, they did not think this would be effective stewardship of resources.
- There was awareness of the needs of the smaller congregations and a discernment that those with greater resources have a responsibility to share their gifts with those with less financial resources.
- Recent experiences of alienation of property and divestiture of buildings and institutions challenged them to examine their attitudes and actions. For instance, two academies in the area, unaware of the other's decision, announced their closing within twenty-four hours of each other.
- Present facilities were stretched to their limits, with waiting lists for accepting new residents.
- They were not making the best use of their resources. In some cases they were all "doing the same thing separately."
- They believed they could provide a better quality care for their members if they were to combine their efforts and resources.
- There is a need for congregations to witness a broader vision of church. Collaboration is a way of doing this.

- They viewed themselves as sisters and brothers in regious life. They are related to each other and share a mutual responsibility for each other.

Obstacles to Collaboration

Sister Marjorie indicated that the obstacles encountered were minimal. She was able to identify a few:

- The decision-making processes and leadership models used by the different congregations sometimes caused tension or delay.
- Since the board members are generally major superiors, the mechanics of getting people together, not surprisingly, sometimes proves difficult. The fact that they perdure is an indication of their conviction of the value of the project.
- The election or appointment of a new leadership team is potentially problematic.

Recommendations to Others Contemplating Such a Project

- Identify a common need, interest, or desire.
- Establish a commitment in faith to live the project.
- Realize that each situation is unique. They discovered that often in similar projects one group is in charge and the oth-ers join in "their" project. This project is "owned" by equal participating members.
- Maintain continuity in board membership.
- Identify the gifts needed in the person chosen to lead the project.
- Realize that there will be setbacks.
- Develop a strong level of trust among all involved. When asked to explain how this had been achieved, Sister Marjorie suggested the following six points:

    1. Individuals exhibited a strong sense of integrity and authenticity of commitment to the group.
    2. There was clarity of focus and role and commitment to a perceived need.
    3. Continuity (the original seven members of the board remain) was maintained.

4. Confidence in the Executive Director was given as a result of clear, comprehensive communication.
5. The board was unanimous in major decisions.
6. There was creative utilization of the resources of the board members and congregations.

Learning Points

Among the learning points gleaned from this interview are the following:

- It takes a great deal of energy to embrace a collaborative approach. There are times when there is a temptation to yield to a more unilateral way.
- The success is dependent on the willingness of all involved to maintain a sense of listening and open-mindedness.
- Given the diversity of personalities involved, it is important to assure that all voices are heard.

Project 2: St. Mary's Parish, Colt Neck, NJ

Interviewee:
   Father William J. Bausch
Address:
   P.O. Box 1068
   Point Pleasant, NJ 08742
Phone:
   732-899-5989
Fax:
   732-892-8848
E-mail:
   ppbbausch@aol.com

Background Information

St. Mary's of Colt Neck, New Jersey, is a parish that has grown in twenty-five years from a handful of members to a parish of over 1,700 families. St. Mary's has been recognized as one of the outstanding parishes in the United States.

Fr. William Bausch was the pastor for twenty-three years prior to his recent retirement. He is the author of over twenty books, most of which are related to his experience of pastoring at St. Mary.

Reason for Being Convinced of the Need for Collaboration

There were two predominate reasons for undertaking collaborative ministry in the parish: theoretical and practical. The theoretical was predicated on the theology that emanated from the Second Vatican Council. This is the theology that describes the church as the people of God. It is based on the conviction that every baptized person is gifted and called to ministry as a result of their reception of the sacraments of baptism and confirmation.

The practical impetus was the need felt by the pastor. As the parish grew, the limits of the pastor became more evident. The gifts of all were needed.

Obstacles to Collaboration

There were two major obstacles encountered in initiating collaborative ministry. The first obstacle was church leadership. The pastor took seriously the prophetic call of the Second Vatican Council. Diocesan leaders did not appear to embrace fully or understand clearly the implications of these new concepts. The pastor found himself implementing the decrees of this Council without tangible support or encouragement from the institutional church.

The second obstacle was the laity. Many Catholics had drifted into a passive role within a paternalistic, hierarchical institution. Thirty years ago only minimal education and catechesis had been available. As a result, the general tendency on the part of many of the faithful was to resist the changes being introduced.

Recommendations to Others Contemplating Developing Intentional Collaborative Ministry in the Parish

There are two major recommendations. First, place an emphasis on catechesis and education. Second, emphasize the spiritual elements.

Catechesis is a slow process that demands immense patience on the part of leaders. Fr. Bausch indicated that it took almost a dozen years before he saw significant changes. A criterion for success is when there is a change in vocabulary. An example given was when the parishioners began to say, "What a beautiful church—and the building is nice too." This was a clear indication that they had grasped the meaning of: we are the church.

There are three key questions that form the essence of parish education: Who are we? Who are we as the people of God? What are we about (mission)?

The responsibility for education and catechesis is not the sole domain of the pastor. This responsibility must be shared by all. Bausch referred to the Glenmary Dance of the Glenmary Missionaries. Glenmary Dance consists of training groups to assume responsibility for ministries and expecting those trained to educate the next generation of ministers. A clear example is when the parishioners began assuming responsibility for leading the Liturgy of the Hours. Initially, the pastor was with the parishioners in the front of the church. Gradually, he moved into the body of the church with the other parishioners. The initial leaders then train the subsequent leaders.

The second recommendation would be to make spirituality a priority. This includes: education for spirituality, providing resources for spiritual growth and spiritual direction, and stressing the spiritual rationale for all parish projects. When spirituality is at the heart of all that transpires within the parish, there is a discernable change in the parish.

Learning Points
- Collaboration transforms parishes.
- When a parish becomes collaborative, the pastor comes to appreciate what it means to be church.
- When collaboration is fostered, life continues even when there is a change of pastors. Pastors come and go. The people are the consistent entity.
- Parishioners experience a sense of joy when they assume their role and responsibility as collaborators.

- People respond enthusiastically when there is good catechesis.
- The pastor becomes a learner when collaboration is prevalent.
- Collaboration works!

Project 3: Washington Middle School for Girls

Interviewee:
Mary Bourdon, RJM, Administrator
Address:
1811 Alabama Ave., S.E.
Washington, DC 20010
Phone:
202-678-1113
Fax:
202-265-1842

Background Information

The Washington Middle School for Girls is an alternative educational institution primarily for African-American girls of middle school age who are at risk for dropping out of school. The school is located in basement rooms of a housing project in the Anacostia area of Washington, D.C. Currently the school is for sixth and seventh graders, with the plan to add more grades when the physical plant will allow expansion. The project is sponsored by three founding organizations: The Society of the Holy Child Jesus, the Religious of Jesus and Mary, and the National Association of Negro Women.

Motivation for Initiating the Project

A group of women introduced through mutual friends joined together to discuss a common interest and area of need. They brainstormed ways they could serve young, economically disadvantaged African-American girls who are at risk of early termination of their education. The group decided they could better do something together rather than as separate individuals or entities. They believed there would be strength in doing a project together. Once they met, they were energized by the mutuality. The number of individuals involved in the initial planning provided a broad base of support that helped the project move forward. The combined efforts gave an excitement to the project.

Reasons for Being Convinced of the Value of Collaboration

There were three main reasons given for being convinced of the value of collaboration:

First, the diversity of the project itself was a positive factor.

Also, the cross-cultural aspect, as well as the various religious affiliations, added a richness.

Finally, the Washington Middle School for Girls is founded "in the spirit of courageous women" Cornelia Connelly, Claudine Thevenet, and Mary McLeod Bethune, the founders of the three organizations now involved with the school. Their combined charisms give a richness of experience that one charism alone could not provide.

Obstacles to Collaboration

Sr. Mary was clear on the obstacles that this collaborative project faced and still continues to address. Mainly, this involves the internal hierarchy of one of the organizations.

The project was initiated by individuals who then needed to gather the support of the organizations to sponsor the project. This was essential. In the beginning the planners were looking for equality in support and commitment, but that doesn't work and is not realistic. Rather, the planners looked for each group to answer on their own the question, "How are you invested in this project?"

Recommendations to Others Contemplating Such a Project

There are two major recommendations:

- Keep the project going even when it is difficult. Don't look at what you don't have, but focus on what benefits you have with collaboration.

- Once the project is underway, the leadership has to be apart from the original three organizations. The project should be established as a separate corporation. The new entity has a life of its own coming from its mission. The three organizations then need to look at how they support the new corporation. A secure structure needs to be in place so as not to lose the organizations and their support. In this project a board of trustees was formed. Each of the founding organizations has a right to place two members on the board. Once the mission is set, the board takes over and the collaboration becomes the vehicle to accomplish the mission.

Learning Points
- Collaboration is well worth it. It is a rich vehicle for the mission. It may feel troublesome in the beginning, but it is energizing.
- Sr. Mary stated simply, "I get excited when I think about the spirit of the three women who founded the three organizations. It becomes the energy for you. Collaboration is a meeting of those three unique spirits."

Observations on Three Church-Related Projects
In reviewing these three projects certain common aspects of collaboration emerge:

- Collaboration generally emerges when there is a perceived need.
- Collaboration is successful when there is conviction in the value of collaboration to respond to that need.
- Problems and snags are inevitable.
- Collaboration evolves through a slow, steady process.
- Collaboration works!

Research in the Non-Church Arena
The Amherst H. Wilder Foundation published the results of a study on the factors which influence successful collaboration. They identify a number of reasons why collaboration is

such a hot topic today. "Going it alone," they declare, does not effect the desired outcomes. However, the driving force behind the explosion of collaboration appears to be financially motivated. Funding agencies are demanding that those agencies that request financial support collaborate because of the conviction that collaboration is the more effective way of delivering services to clients.

In *Collaboration: What Makes It Work: A Review of Factors Influencing Successful Collaboration*, the authors define collaboration as,

> A mutually beneficial and well-defined relationship entered into by two or more organizations to achieve common goals.

This definition would certainly describe the reality of the three examples cited in this chapter.

The report reviewed case study reports of collaboration and focused on the following questions:

- What are the ingredients of successful collaboration?
- What differentiates the successful from the unsuccessful projects?
- What contributes to the success of collaboration?

The report identifies the key elements of successful collaboration based on the review of the case studies. We present the eleven elements (Table 11.1) that were identified in five or more studies. Most of the findings are predictable. However, logical realities are often overlooked. Those elements can serve as an ideal for developing criteria for initiating collaborative projects.

Table 11.1	*Factors Influencing the Success of Collaboration*
	1. A history of collaboration exists.
	2. Mutual respect, understanding, and trust are present.
	3. The collaborative venture is composed of an appropriate cross section of members.
	4. Members see collaboration in their self-interest.
	5. Members share a stake in both the process and outcome.

Table 11.1 *(cont.)*	6. There are multiple layers of decision-making. 7. Open and frequent communication is the norm. 8. Informal and formal communication links are established. 9. There are concrete attainable goals and objectives. 10 There are sufficient funds for the project. 11. A skilled convener leads them.

The Existence of a History of Collaboration

The fact that the participants had a previous history of collaboration has an influence on the outcome: roles and expectations are more realistic, and there is a pre-condition for trust, especially a trust in the process. Positive experiences produce positive beliefs. The less the prior experience of collaboration, the greater the amount of "ground work" required.

Mutual Respect, Understanding, and Trust

Common sense dictates that when the individuals involved have a mutual respect for each other, combined with a reciprocal level of understanding and trust, any effort is almost certain of success.

Taking time to get to know each other is not wasted time, but rather sacred moments on which positive relationships are developed.

Appropriate Cross Section of Members

Like many of the findings, appropriate cross section of membership can be characterized as common sense. However, common sense is often the least common commodity. The research cautions against an attempt to become overly inclusive. Developing a client base which is too large or too broad condemns a project to failure. Among the recommendations of the study are: involve those who are essential for the success of the project, include those who have the power and control to assure success, continually determine which new groups or gifts are required, and provide an adequate orientation program for those who are not involved from the beginning.

Members See Collaboration in Their Self-Interest

Since most human behavior is need-directed, it is imperative that participants see personal value in what is being undertaken. In Christian groups the "self-interest" does not have to be narcissistic. Rather this self-interest can be tantamount to the furthering of the gospel or the spiritual goals of the organization.

Members Share Stake in Both Process and Outcome

The criteria identified here is "ownership." Until the participants truly feel this sense of ownership, their commitment will be, at best, ambivalent. The ownership must be of both the process and the product. Failure to develop a strong sense of ownership assures failure.

Multiple Layers of Decision-Making

The more varied the layers of decision-making included in the process, the greater the chance of success. Projects which develop realistic ways to involve leadership, management, and those at the level of delivery of service are more likely to succeed.

Open and Frequent Communication

Communication in productive collaborative endeavors is characterized by communication that is open, frequent, clearly defined, and complete. Open, successful communication does not imply the absence of tension and conflict. However, when communication systems have been developed which allow for appropriate "airings" of difficult issues, better collaboration will occur.

Formal and Informal Communication Links

Communication is never perfect. However, it has greater possibilities for success when: there are clear structures developed; a method for evaluating, refining, and assuring accountability is programmed into the process; and when the preferred method of communication is face-to-face, rather than paper or electronic communication. The more personal the communication the greater the opportunities to quickly correct miscommunications and misconceptions. The research suggests that stable representation or consistency in the key people involved is a way to assure good communication.

Concrete Attainable Goals and Objectives

Projects have the greatest potential for success when the goals and objectives are clear, realistic, and shared. Ambiguity will create problems. It helps when there are both short-term and long-term goals. Regular evaluation of progress toward goals and objectives is strongly recommended.

Sufficient Funds

Not many church projects have sufficient funds. This is an ideal. When the funding is insufficient often the energy is inordinately directed at securing funds and is diverted from the goals and objectives.

Skilled Convener

The more skilled the convener, the more likely the energy of the group will be expended in valuable pursuits. Skilled conveners may be at a premium. This is why good communication and collaboration can assist in locating resources to assist in any collaborative project.

Conclusions

We invite the reader to reflect on the same questions we raised to the interviewees.

- What motivated the people who began this program?
- Why are you convinced of the need for collaboration?
- What are the greatest obstacles encountered?
- From your experience what would you recommend to others?
- What have you learned about collaboration from this experience?

Sharing responses with others involved in the same collaborative project can reap valuable data for continued dialogue and growth.

Epilogue

Collaborative Leadership:
A Challenge to All

Arriving at a parish to conduct a workshop, we were greeted by the director of religious education who asked if we had met the pastor. She then began to enumerate his shortcomings, stressing his lack of collaboration and need to control. Given this information, we were less than eager to meet him! Before we had that opportunity, we encountered some parishioners who likewise inquired if we had met the pastor. However, their impressions differed dramatically from the DRE's. After describing the pastor in complimentary terms, they wondered if we had met the DRE. The parishioners then proceeded to tell us how difficult it was to work with this controlling, non-collaborative person!

The above scenario is not an isolated instance. It demonstrates a common experience when evaluating collaboration. The tendency is to focus on the shortcomings of others and to place blame outside of self, rather than admit one's own inadequacies. The only person I can change is myself. Collaborative ministry will become more authentic when more energy is directed toward changing me rather than in trying to change others.

We end this book with challenges and questions to those in various leadership roles. Collaboration is possible only when each collaborator is willing to engage in the difficult and, at times, painful personal reflection, assessment, and conversion.

We hope each person will read the challenges as addressed to herself and himself. Self-deception, which blocks conversion in one's life, can be a very definite obstacle to collaboration. Like the DRE in the above story, it is easy to be acutely aware of the speck in another's eye but completely oblivious to the beam in our own.

Hierarchy

If you are in church hierarchy, do you embrace your role as leaders of the collaborative church? This role requires you to teach, to model, to challenge, and to establish the structures for facilitating collaborative ministry at every level of the church.

Cardinal Mahony challenges all leaders, including those in the hierarchy, to use their authority to provide opportunities for individuals to employ their God-given gifts in ministry (PAL, p. 19).

The hierarchy can only call others to be collaborative if they, themselves, model collaboration in their leadership. The words of Pope Paul VI are especially pertinent to the hierarchy:

> Modern man listens more willingly to witnesses than to teachers, and if he does listen to teachers, it is because they are witnesses (EN).

It is the diocesan bishop who has the authority to make decisions which will facilitate collaboration. Among his options are: (1) arranging for and mandating programs to sensitize and train all ministers in the diocese for collaboration; (2) establishing priorities within the budget which reward those departments who function most collaboratively; (3) establishing diocesan offices and providing resources to foster the ongoing development of collaborative efforts; (4) assuring that collaboration is an integral part of all formation programs within the diocese; and (5) creating methods for accountability. We encourage each bishop to reflect on the following:

- Am I convinced that a more collaborative style of ministry gives a positive direction to the church's mission?
- How willing am I to use my authority and resources to establish the structures necessary to develop the diocese as a more collaborative church?
- Do the people who work at the diocesan level model collaboration between departments? If not, do I intervene?
- How am I perceived as a collaborative leader? How can I discern whether my perception matches that of the people in the chancery and the larger population of the diocese? How open am I to receiving such feedback?

Deacons

Deacons and the larger diaconate community have a specific and vital role to play in the collaborative church. Pope Paul VI, in reestablishing the diaconate, clearly indicated that one of the primary reasons for doing so was to create a group of ministers whose primary responsibility is to animate the rest of the Christian community for ministry and service. He describes the deacon as an "instimulator" with ministerial responsibility "to be the animator and promoter of the church's service in the local community." Deacons have a special commission to animate and empower the gifts of others and to model collaborative ministry for all in the church (CPG).

Bishop Hubbard explained that one of the primary roles of deacons is to give power to the laity:

> [Deacons] should be an advocate for the laity where they are unable to speak for themselves. Otherwise, the deacons' efforts can be very self-serving, and as discriminatory towards the laity as some clergy and religious have been and still tend to be (GPP).

We invite the members of the diaconate community to reflect on the following:

- Do I perceive the animation of gifts of the entire Christian community to be a major focus of diaconal ministry?
- Did my training and preparation prepare me with the attitude and skills to be an animator?

- How can deacons more fully embrace this prophetic vision of *diakonia*?

Laity

The future success of collaborative ministry is more dependent on the laity than on any other group in the church.

Among the venues for the laity's ministry are the workplace, the home, and the neighborhood. In those places the laity are in a unique position to transform the world and bring the presence of Christ into every seemingly mundane activity.

Collaboration is only fully possible when we utilize all the gifts present within the Christian community. The anemia and ennui present in the church will diminish when more laity recognize their gifts and respond to the call to mission.

The collaborative church does not only need lay ministers. It requires lay *leaders*. The skills and insights gleaned by laity in their homes and workplaces provide them with a rich source of giftedness which is needed within the church.

We pose some questions for the laity's reflection:

- Do I value my ministry in the home and workplace as much as I value the ministries in the church?
- What personal responsibility am I assuming for the continued development of my gifts?
- What initiative do I take in continuing to challenge and affirm church leaders?
- Do I allow my frustration with the institution church to marginalize me from the church?

Priests

Priests are in a unique position to facilitate or hinder the development of collaborative ministry, especially at the parish level. Becoming more collaborative will reap not only ministerial results, but also benefits for the clergy. First, much of the stress and burnout experienced by clergy could be alleviated by a more collaborative approach to ministry. Second, to the degree that priests become more collaborative, they are free to be the priests they want to be and the church needs them to be. As others assume ministerial roles, priests can direct their attention and energy to their role as spiritual leader, the minister of word and sacrament. They can be liberated to shed many of the ministries and responsibilities which can be adequately performed by others.

When clergy foster the development of collaborative ministry and empower the gifts of others, the members of the parish will become more life-filled and the parish will become more life-giving. It is an all-win, no-lose situation. This empowering of the gifts of the laity is of the very essence of the priesthood:

> . . . the ministerial priesthood is at the service of the common priesthood. It is directed at the unfolding of the baptismal grace of all Christians (CCC #1547).

Clergy also have the opportunity through their corporate strength as a presbyterate to lobby for what is needed to develop a more collaborative diocesan church.

The following reflection questions are offered for priests:

- Do I want to see the parish become more collaborative or am I fearful that such a move will weaken my "power" within the parish?
- How willing am I to initiate, endorse, and fund whatever is needed to make our parish more collaborative?
- What retraining do I need to become more collaborative?

Religious Women and Men

Many religious provided the leadership for the renewal which came in the wake of the Second Vatican Council. Now the challenge is to discover new ways to be prophetic in fostering the gifts of the entire people of God.

We are at a point in history where competent religious, like the Lord, himself, must turn over the mission to others. Laity are being trained and prepared to move into those ministries which were previously the distinctive realm of religious.

The challenge to religious is to extricate themselves from ministries where laity are prepared. In addition, religious women and men must advocate the development, not only of lay associates, but of lay leaders.

The following questions are offered for men and women religious:

- Do I believe that I can learn and benefit from the gifts of laity and, especially, the diocesan clergy?
- How willing am I, like John the Baptist, to decrease so that others may increase?
- How can I be prophetic in fostering the gifts of others?

A Last Word

In concluding we raise a final question for the reader:
How are you being called to become more collaborative?

Bibliography

The following are the books, articles, and documents quoted or referred to in this document. Church documents are listed under Sources (pages 186-189).

Burghardt, Walter J., SJ. *Seasons That Laugh and Weep*. Mahwah, NJ: Paulist Press, 1983.

Burkert, William and Loughlan Sofield. "Unwrapping Your Gifts," *Human Development*, Vol. 7, # 2, Summer 1986, pp. 43-46.

Castelli, Jim and Joseph Gremillion. *The Emerging Parish: The Notre Dame Study of Catholic Life Since Vatican II*. San Francisco: Harper & Row, 1987.

Erikson, Erik. *Childhood and Society*. New York: W. W. Norton and Co., 1963.

Fenhagen, James C. *Invitation to Holiness*. San Francisco: Harper & Row, 1985.

Friedman, Edwin H. "Emotional Process in the Marketplace: The Family Therapist as Consultant with Work Systems," in McDaniel, Susan, Lyman Wynn, and Timothy Weber. *Systems Consultation: A New Perspective for Families*. New York, NY: Guilford, 1986.

Gault, Stanley C. "A Commitment to Competitiveness," *American Way*. April 1, 1987, p. 18.

Gill, James. "Burnout: A Growing Threat in Ministry," *Human Development*. Vol. 1, No. 1, Summer 1980, pp. 21-27.

Harris, Maria. *Proclaim Jubilee! A Spirituality for the Twenty-First Century*. Louisville, KY: Westminster John Knox Press, 1996.

Hubbard, Howard J. *Fulfilling the Vision: Collaborative Ministry in the Parish*. New York: Crossroad, 1998.

Leege, David. "Parish Life Among the Leaders," *Notre Dame Study on Catholic Parish Life*. Report #9. Notre Dame: University of Notre Dame, December, 1986.

Mattessich, Paul and Barbara Monsey. *Collaboration: What Makes It Work: A Review of Factors Influencing Successful Collaboration.* St. Paul, MN: The Wilder Foundation, 1992.

McNeill, Donald, Douglas Morrison, and Henri Nouwen. *Compassion: A Reflection on the Christian Life.* Garden City, NY: Image Books, 1983.

Merton, Thomas. *Seeds of Contemplation.* Norfolk, CT: New Direction Books, 1949.

Morris, Deborah. *Forgiving the Dead Man Walking.* Grand Rapids, MI: Zondervan, 1998.

Murnion, Philip J., et al. *New Parish Ministers.* New York: National Pastoral Life Center, 1992.

_____. *New Parish Ministry: Laity and Religious on Parish Staff.* New York: National Pastoral Life Center, 1992.

Murnion, Philip J. and David DeLambo. *Parishes and Parish Ministers: A Study of Parish Lay Ministry.* New York: National Pastoral Life Center, 1999.

National Opinion Research Center. *The Catholic Priest in the United States: Sociological Investigations.* Washington, DC: United States Catholic Conference, 1972.

Nouwen, Henri. *The Wounded Healer.* Garden City, NY: Doubleday, 1972.

Satir, Virginia. *Conjoint Family Therapy.* Palo Alto: Science and Behavior Books, 1967.

Searles, Harold. *Collected Papers on Schizophrenia and Related Subjects.* New York: International Universities Press, 1965.

Sofield, Loughlan. "Building a Pastoral Council," *Today's Parish.* April/May 1988, pp. 22-24.

Sofield, Loughlan and Carroll Juliano. *Collaborative Ministry: Skills and Guidelines.* Notre Dame: Ave Maria Press, 1987.

_____. "Developing a Pastoral Council," *Today's Parish.* April/May 1987, pp. 17-19.

Sofield, Loughlan, Rosine Hammett, and Carroll Juliano. *Building Community: Christian, Caring, Vital.* Notre Dame: Ave Maria Press, 1998.

_____. *Design for Wholeness*. Notre Dame: Ave Maria Press, 1990.

Sofield, Loughlan and Donald Kuhn. *The Collaborative Leader: Listening to the Wisdom of God's People*. Notre Dame: Ave Maria Press, 1995. pp. 90-92.

Walker, Leonore. *The Battered Woman*. New York: Harper & Row, 1979.

Sources

The following are church documents that are quoted in this book. The abbreviations designate each document within the text.

AA   *Decree on the Apostolate of the Laity (Aposticam Actuosiatatem)*.

ALA   John Paul II. *Ad Limina Apostolorum to the Bishops Conference of France* on January 25, 1997.

BMC   Archdiocese of Brisbane. *Becoming More Collaborative*.

CCC   *Catechism of the Catholic Church*. Washington, DC: U.S. Catholic Conference, 1995.

CCS   *Common Curriculum in Catholic Schools*. Committee of Catholic School Boards of Ontario, published by Institute for Catholic Education, Toronto, 1995.

CFL   John Paul II. *The Vocation and Mission of the Lay Faithful in the Church and in the World (Christifideles Laici)*. Washington, DC: U. S. Catholic Conference, 1988.

CG   National Conference of Catholic Bishops. *Called and Gifted for the Third Millennium: Reflections of the U.S. Catholic Bishops on the Thirtieth Anniversary of the Decree on the Apostolate of the Laity and the Fifteenth Anniversary of Called and Gifted*. Washington, DC: NCCB/USCC, 1995.

CMW   Vatican Council II. *Pastoral Constitution on the Church in the Modern World (Gaudium et Spes)*.

CPG   Paul VI. *Pacedeum, Apostlic Letter of Pope Paul VI*, August 15, 1972.

CTH   John Paul II. *Crossing the Threshold of Hope*, p. 128.

CTM   John Paul II. *On the Coming of the Third Millennium*. Apostolic Letter, November 10, 1994.

ELM   Howard J. Hubbard, "Reflections on the Experience of Ecclesial Lay Ministry," A paper presented at a Conference of Ecclesial Lay Ministries, sponsored by the Subcommittee of Ecclesial Lay Ministry of the Committee of Laity, Women, Family and Youth of the United States National Conference of Catholic Bishops, May 1997.

EN   Pope Paul VI. *On Evangelization in the Modern World (Evangelii Nuntiandi)*. Washington, DC: U.S. Catholic Conference, 1976.

FWD   Committee on Women in Society and in the Church, National Conference of Catholic Bishops. *From Words to Deeds: Continuing Reflections on the Role of Women in the Church*. Washington, DC: U.S. Catholic Conference, 1998.

GPP   Hubbard, Howard J. "We Are God's Priestly People: A Vision for the Church of Albany in the 1990's," *The Evangelist*, October 20, 1988.

GU   National Conference of Catholic Bishops, Committee on the Laity. *Gifts Unfolding: The Lay Vocation Today With Questions for Tomorrow*. Washington, DC: U. S. Catholic Conference, 1990.

HG   Pope John Paul II. A homily he gave in Glasgow, Scotland, June 1, 1992.

J2   Subcommittee on the Third Millennium. *Jubilee 2000: A Year of the Lord's Favor: A Reflection on Forgiveness and Reconciliation*. National Conference of Catholic Bishops/United States Catholic Conference. Washington, DC. November, 1998.

LAB   Third General Conference of Latin American Bishops. *Evangelization at Present and in the Future of Latin America*. Conclusions. Pueblo, 1979.

LCW   Apostola, Nicholas (ed). *A Letter from Christ to the World*. World Council of Churches. Geneva, 1998.

MC   Bishops Committee on the Liturgy, National Conference of Catholic Bishops. *Study Text III: Ministries in the Church: Commentary on the Apostolic Letters of Pope Paul VI, Misisteria quaedam and Ad pascendum*. United States Catholic Conference. Washington, DC, 1974.

MR   Pope John Paul II. *Mission of the Redeemer (Redemptoris Missio)*. Encyclical Letter, 1991.

NCP   Howard J. Hubbard. "A Vision for Parish Planning and Re-structuring," *Origins*. 25:726-736, April 11, 1996.

NE   Pope John Paul II. "Opening Address of the Holy Father," *New Evangelization, Human Development, Christian Culture*. Fourth General Conference of Latin American Bishops. Santo Domingo, Dominican Republic, Oct. 12-18, 1992.

PAL   Roger Mahony. *Priests and Laity: Mutual Empowerment*. A pastoral letter (undated).

PLL   Catholic Bishops of Florida. *Pastoral Letter to the Laity*. May 19, 1991.

PPC   Canadian Conference of Catholic Bishops. *The Parish Pastoral Council*. 1985.

RDE   Congregation of Christian Education. *Religious Dimension of Education in Catholic Schools*. 1998.

ROL   Roger Mahony. *Pastoral Letter on the Role of the Laity in the Life of the Archdiocese of Los Angeles*. A pastoral letter issued on December 3, 1986.

RP   William Borders. "You Are A Royal Priesthood," *Origins*. Vol. 18, No. 11, August 18, 1988.

SDL   National Conference of Catholic Bishops. *Sons and Daughters of the Light: Ministry with Young Adults: A National Pastoral Plan*. United States Catholic Conference, Inc. Washington, DC, 1996.

SOF   Archdiocese of Brisbane. *Shaping Our Future*. (undated)

SV   John Paul II. *Splendor Veritatis*, Encyclical Letter, August 6, 1993.

SWG   Bishops' Conference of England and Wales. *The Sign We Give: Report from the Working Party on Collaborative Ministry*. September, 1995.

TWH   National Catholic Educational Association, National Conference of Catechetical Leadership and United States Catholic Conference, Department of Education (A Collaborative Effort). *Those Who Hear You Hear Me: A Resource for Bishops and Diocesan Educational/Catechetical Leaders.* United States Catholic Conference, Inc. Washington, DC, 1995.

WTC   Kenneth Himes. This material was presented at the Woodstock Theological Center, Georgetown University, June 1995. The presentation was part of a forum, "The Church in the Modern World: A Thirty Year Perspective," and was reported in *Woodstock Report*, #42.

Br. Loughlan Sofield, ST, a leading consultant on ministry and personal development, lectures and gives workshops across the United States as well as internationally. His two most recent books (both from Ave Maria Press) were awarded first place by the Catholic Press Association: *Building Community: Christian, Caring, Vital* co-authored with Rosine Hammett and Carroll Juliano, and *The Collaborative Leader* co-authored with Donald Kuhn. He is senior editor of *Human Development* magazine and a member of the Missionary Servants of the Most Holy Trinity.

Sr. Carroll Juliano, SHCJ, a member of the Society of the Holy Child Jesus, is currently serving on the congregation's formation team of the American Province. Her background in education includes teaching, administration, and career counseling. She has offered presentations throughout the United States, Canada, Asia, Europe, Africa, and Australia. Carroll has authored numerous articles and books. She is co-author of *Building Community: Christian, Caring, Vital; Design for Wholeness: Dealing with Anger, Learning to Forgive;* and *Building Self-Esteem.* In 1999 *Building Community* was awarded first place by the Catholic Press Association in the category of professional books.

Other titles of interest...

BUILDING COMMUNITY
Christian, Caring, Vital
Loughlan Sofield, ST, Carroll Juliano, SHCJ, and Rosine Hammett, CSC
A practical workbook that describes the developmental stages of community, provides a model for understanding the inter-dynamics in a community and explores beliefs about community directly affecting its development. / $11.95*

DESIGN FOR WHOLENESS
Dealing with Anger, Learning to Forgive, Building Self-Esteem
Loughlan Sofield ST, Carroll Juliano, SHCJ, and Rosine Hammett, CSC
The authors present a model and a case study for understanding and dealing with anger, a discussion of forgiveness and propose a model for understanding and increasing self-esteem. / $8.95*

THE COLLABORATIVE LEADER
Listening to the Wisdom of God's People
Loughlan Sofield, ST and Donald H. Kuhn
Foreword by Dolores Leckey
How can church leaders be more competent, dynamic and effective? Based on interviews with 42 lay Christian leaders in diverse fields. The answer is collaboration. They stress that the collaborative leader is a person of character who listens, responds to needs, establishes a vision and empowers others to use their gifts and abilities. / $9.95*

THE WORKPLACE
Christians Tell Their Stories
Loughlan Sofield, ST and Donald H. Kuhn
Kuhn and Sofield pose challenging questions to Christians in the workplace who want to integrate their spirituality, their world and their roles as Christians. These interviews contribute a powerful witness about how others live and celebrate their Christian values and beliefs while being fully involved in the world of work. audiocassette, $8.95*

SELF-ESTEEM AND CHRISTIAN GROWTH
Loughlan Sofield, ST
The Christian response to the gospel call to holiness, community, and ministry, depends on healthy self-esteem. This is the message Sofield brings us. He offers criteria for self-evaluation. He suggests numerous ways people can increase their self-esteem even as they lower their levels of competition and hostility. / audiocassette, $7.95*

* prices subject to change

These titles may be purchased at your bookstore. To request a complete catalog contact
AmP Ave Maria Press / PO Box 428 / Notre Dame, Indiana 46556-0428
1-800-282-1865 / E-mail:avemariapress.1@nd.edu / www.avemariapress.com